Why Aren't You More Like Me?

STYLES & SKILLS FOR LEADING & LIVING WITH CREDIBILITY

EVERETT T. ROBINSON
Co-author of the *Personal Style Indicator*

SECOND EDITION

Sumas, Washington

This book is dedicated to:

- ***Pam***, my "little girl" and favorite interior designer
- ***Ron***, the son who moves to the beat of a different drum
- ***Jeramy***, a certified Led Zepplin specialist
- ***Pam***, Jeramy's very own Mad Hatter

and above all, ***Denise***,
my main Love, Best Friend, and Eternal Companion.

I love you all.

CONTENTS

Part One: DEVELOP CREDIBILITY BY LEADING WITH STYLE

Part Two: THE FUNDAMENTALS OF PERSONAL STYLE

CONTENTS

CONTENTS

CONTENTS

LIST OF CHARTS

Foreword

By Terry Anderson, Ph.D.
Co-author of the *Personal Style Indicator* (PSI)

Nobody is more qualified to write this book than Everett Robinson. No one else has delivered more training sessions, more workshops, more seminars, and more classes using the PSI. It is unlikely that anyone else could supply such a clearly organized account of personal style theory or present such a sensitive rendering of this theory's significance for improving interpersonal communication and relationships at work and at home.

Among Everett's strengths is his facility for helping others understand a potentially complex subject—a strength that is sustained throughout his writing. He consistently displays the unique ability to communicate how theory applies to the personal domain, illuminating how people's preferred styles of interaction can be such key factors in every experience of their lives. The manifold examples he provides in these pages reflect his background in presenting personal style theory to a wide variety of audiences, from chief executive officers to high school students. Exceeding in richness and applicability, the examples included in the Second Edition testify to Everett's ongoing concern that people learn how this theory can make a difference in their lives and benefit from it.

The need for this book is rooted in the basic desire to understand and improve the self, as is the need for the PSI, which itself has created a demand for information on personal style theory. Frequently, when people first encounter the PSI, they are astonished by its power and simplicity. Many of them later express deeply felt gratitude for the way the tool has enriched their lives. They become fascinated by the concept of personal style because it has helped them to understand themselves better and to gain insight into the problems they experience with co-workers, colleagues, friends, and family members.

Even after attending seminars and workshops on personal style, people often ask for more information about the theory underlying this concept, and there have been a multitude of requests for further guidance on how to apply a knowledge of personal style in daily life—which is how it should be. The PSI was never intended to be more than a beginning; it is not a panacea. Self-development is achieved by individuals struggling to gain more control over their lives, to assume more responsibility for their actions, and to cultivate more tolerance for the differences between people.

Self-development need not be a solitary struggle, however, *Why Aren't You More Like Me?* acts as a vital link in a diverse, far-ranging community of individuals engaged in this struggle; moreover, it provides the general reader with a much needed introduction to what personal style is and how an awareness of its influence can help each one of us. It offers a very unique kind of assistance, picking up where the PSI left off.

Unlike many previous discussions of the differences between people, Everett's presentation moves well beyond simply describing what these differences are. His focus sharpens and probes deeper, trying to account for why they exist. He concentrates on the practical value of recognizing these distinctions, and he reveals how developing personal style versatility and acquiring the skills of "style-shifting" can lead us to experience more satisfying relationships with others.

Readers who are familiar with Everett's work will be pleased to discover that the Second Edition of this book is even friendlier and more encouraging of personal growth than the previous edition. If you have completed the PSI, have hungered for more information about personal style theory and its application, and are encountering Everett's writing for the first time, this text will provide what you've been waiting to devour. If you are not acquainted with the PSI and personal style theory, you will find that this book offers a stimulating opportunity to begin a journey of self-exploration and self-development.

Whatever your experience, these pages can inspire you to become more of the person you have the potential to be. I trust that your reading and application of the knowledge gained from *Why Aren't You More Like Me?* will be a truly enriching experience.

Acknowledgements

As with the writing of any book, many people are involved besides the author. While my name alone appears on the cover, there are several individuals to whom I would like to express special thanks for each has contributed in a significant way to the completion of this book. Whatever faults remain, they would have been more numerous without the assistance, guidance, and support of the following individuals.

First of all, I want to thank **Terry Anderson**, founder and chairman of The Consulting Resource Group International, Inc. (CRG), for the inspiration, creativity, and friendship he has offered me since we first met many years ago. He helped me finally see the missing pieces I was looking for, both in terms of personality and spirituality. He also strongly encouraged me to write the book, and some of the information it presents was developed with his assistance. I also want to thank him for allowing me to collaborate with him in the development of the Personal Style Indicator, the In-Depth Pattern Interpretations, and with many other educational materials published by CRG.

I would also like to specially thank **Ted James** for coming to my assistance when I thought I would never get the original version of this book finished. His editorial help and comments on the structure of the First Edition were most needed and appreciated. His keen eye for detail and organization have greatly improved what I was originally intending to print.

For the Second Edition of the book, I would like to express appreciation to the following people for their assistance in updating and improving the original text:

Marilyn Hamilton for her contributions in the content analysis and publishing contract areas.

Ken Keis for his inspiration and friendship while eating pizzas, and for marketing my books.

Eleanor Parkinson for her cheeriness and superb organizational and administration skills.

Barb Enns for her red pen and its highlights of the many grammatical mistakes, and the many hours she took reading and editing this version.

Karen Young for her desktop publishing expertise and patience with my high-C requests.

Judy Douglas for her excellent effort and spirit when packaging and shipping my books.

Bob Carkhuff and all of his staff at HRD Press for their support and efforts to make my book a success.

Mary George for her editorial efforts on the Second Edition.

I especially want to thank my family for the patience they showed and all the support they provided while I was working on the different drafts the manuscript went through. Much of the time that I could have spent with Denise, Pam, and Jeramy was absorbed in the original production of this text.

Lastly, but most importantly, I shall be forever grateful to **Jesus Christ,** whose love inspired me to care enough about you to write this book. I pray that everyone who reads this book will come to know him as I do.

INTRODUCTION

*Life is like a jigsaw puzzle but you don't have
the picture on the front of the box to know what
it's supposed to look like. Sometimes, you're
not even sure if you have all the pieces.*

— **Roger Von Oech**

A Hidden Piece to the Puzzle

While I am very glad that people are so wonderously unique, I am still often amazed by how we all behave so differently from one another. Why aren't you more like me? And why aren't I more like you?

I've been asking these questions for as long as I can remember, wondering what could possibly account for the differences among people and trying to find some satisfactory explanations. Even after receiving a master's degree in psychology, I lacked the clarity I wanted to achieve. Understanding human behavior has always seemed like putting a jigsaw puzzle together—with a key piece missing.

The search to find this lost piece was frustrating because I didn't really know what I was looking for. I couldn't put a name to it. At times I wasn't even sure I would recognize it if I found it. Now, looking back on my life, I realize I must have tripped over this mysterious piece many times while growing up: it wasn't missing, just hidden. And curiously enough, although like an invisible object it remained concealed, persistently out of reach, I was still aware of its presence in myself and in others.

When I was growing up, my best friend Dave and I did everything together that close friends do. We were inseparable. We shared much in common, but what fascinated me was how different we were. For example, I always "choked" when under pressure; instead of hitting the

1

right musical notes at the annual band concert or making the winning shot in the all-important basketball match, I'd tighten up and flunk the opportunity. But not Dave—he'd shine brightest when the spotlight was on him.

The contrast was due to more than just a difference in ability, although he definitely had more talent in music and athletics than I did. There were also key differences in how we reacted to the changing environment around us. Dave actually seemed to prefer being under pressure. It excited him and inspired him to take up the challenge. He clearly liked standing in front of a crowd and being the focus of everyone's attention—something I couldn't bear. I was more comfortable watching from the sidelines. Whereas he loved to mix with everyone, always eager to meet new people and pleased to see anyone who happened to tag along, I preferred the company of a few people and was annoyed whenever a gang of others burst in and spoiled the intimacy of a small group.

There was also a key distinction in our mental outlooks. Dave was casual, even comical, about everything that I took so seriously. I used to watch him and try to figure out how he remained so calm and unflustered when faced with problems that had me tossing and turning all night. When I asked him about it once, he merely replied, "Well, I don't take time to think about it like you do. When the time comes, I just do it."

Dave was right: I was always dwelling on things, poking at them, prying them open and examining what they contained. I enjoyed living in my mind, mulling over the events of the day, trying to fathom the secrets of the universe. I would analyze what was happening around me and try to predict what would happen next. I wanted to be prepared so I didn't mess anything up when events happened. But Dave was laid-back; he took each day as it came. "Why aren't you more like me?" his behavior seemed to ask. And I used to wonder why I wasn't.

Different yet Similar

Dave and I had different personal styles—that insight was the hidden puzzle piece I'd been looking for, but I didn't realize it until much later. For years I'd been searching for something that would help me become more like other people or help them become more like me. This was the source of the problem. I was looking at the differences between people and trying to remove them rather than accepting them for what they were: just plain differences.

The realization that I needed to accept these differences suddenly opened up a new perspective on life for me. By learning to tolerate—even relish—human diversity, I came to accept myself more. I grew as a person. I learned to develop my talents and realize more of my potential. I stopped worrying about the things I couldn't change and began to focus on the things I could. By letting go of my old self, I didn't find a new self, I found my true self. If this sounds paradoxical that's because it is. The irony of the situation is that when we accept ourselves as we really are, we are afforded our greatest chance of changing.

Slowly I began to notice that the differences between people actually accommodated certain similarities and that these similarities had some consistencies to them. Before long, I was reading avidly, searching now for ways to account for these similarities, among the differences. Eventually, Terry Anderson, a close friend and associate, helped me understand what he had gleaned from a similar search about style differences.

Terry had already examined a number of existing theories about "personality type." We had long discussions about why each was incomplete or seemed biased. We explored ways in which a number of similar approaches could be integrated into a single broader model of "personal style." Together we began to develop a theoretical perspective from which we could better interpret the patterns of differences and similarities that exist between people. This perspective soon grew into the Personal Style Model and then into personal style theory. We then used this model and theory as the background to develop the ***Personal Style Indicator (PSI).****

The PSI was accepted immediately and made a powerful impact. Many people wanted to learn more about our model and the theory behind it, which led us to providing seminars. At the end of these seminars, people often asked for more information. They wanted to know how our model and theory could be used to build significant relationships. I then realized that I needed to write a book about the benefits of understanding personal style theory and applying it to relationships at work and at home.

* If you haven't completed a copy of the PSI, you may want to turn to the Appendix, which contains a mini-version of the PSI. Follow the instructions for completing it so that you will know what your scores and patterns are as you read through the book.

WHY AREN'T YOU MORE LIKE ME?

Why aren't you more like me? Why aren't I more like you? Why aren't we more like each other? These aren't easy questions to answer, but there are reasons for our human differences. I hope you will find the answers you are looking for as you read on, so you can know why you and others are unique. And knowing is where learning and change really begin.

PART ONE

DEVELOP CREDIBILITY BY LEADING WITH STYLE

Chapter 1.
The Search for Personal Style

Unless you know what it is, I ain't never going to be able to explain it to you.
— **Louis Armstrong**

I searched for so long to find some way of explaining why other people I met tended to be so different from me. They appeared similar enough on the surface, but underneath they seemed to think and behave in ways quite opposite from mine. I couldn't understand how they could perceive the same environment so differently. They picked up signals I couldn't read and put importance on matters that I ignored. They also ignored things that I responded to more strongly. What made me angry didn't seem to phase them, and what irritated them had little or no effect on me. All in all, the differences were quite a mystery to me.

Yet, after much observation and head-scratching, I began to notice that the way other people behaved wasn't quite as mysterious as it appeared to be, especially when they were under stress or emotionally upset. Their behavior seemed to fall into some intriguing patterns, and these patterns appeared to reflect certain basic preferences we have for dealing with the world around us.

There were people who were productive and energetic: doers. They always seemed to be focusing on results and how to get them. They were bold, direct, and when they needed to be, authoritative. Then there were the individuals who were analysts, always checking through any available information. These thinker types identified problems, perceived trends, and offered solutions. They were careful calculators who often seemed overly worried about life's events.

In contrast, there were others who appeared less serious. They were verbally persuasive. They could influence people around them with their creative ideas and joking personalities. Always the center of attention, these individuals were the loudest and most off-the-wall when it came to doing anything. Finally, there were the easy going people whose feet were firmly planted on the ground. They were consistent team players, always encouraging others and helping where help was needed. They were the quiet types who were friendly and accepted everyone.

> *If we could first know where we are and whither we are tending, we could better judge what to do and how to do it.*
>
> **— Abraham Lincoln**

The Value of Knowing About Personal Style

I was once lost in a city I was somewhat familiar with, trying to locate a person I wanted to see. I had the person's home address and asked for directions from a gas station attendant, who couldn't help me. I kept searching, even buying a city map and using it to narrow my movements to one specific area, but I still couldn't find the person's house. Finally, I called him and told him where I was. It turned out that I was very close to where he lived, and I quickly joined him; nonetheless, despite my close proximity to my goal, I would have remained lost had I not called him. Even though I had valuable information to assist me in my search, I would have missed the meeting with my friend if I hadn't appealed for help from someone who could tell me what I needed to know.

Life is for learning, and the sooner we ask for the guidance we need, the quicker we can gain the knowledge required to meet our goals. The same holds true for our relationships with ourselves. Although we may recognize the need to know who we are, there is often a part of our personalities that is close to us but impossible to reach without assistance. For many people, this part of the personality is called "personal style."

The better you know yourself, the easier you can decide what you want to accomplish in life. Appreciating how personal style influences your behavior is an important step toward gaining more control over your actions. Understanding how deeply personal style can affect your life opens the door to new opportunities for living and working more successfully. Of key significance, however, is the way personal style theory also encourages you to know others as they really are rather than concentrating on how you wish them to be.

If there is any one secret of sucess, it lies in the ability to get the other person's point of view and see things from his angle as well as your own.

— **Henry Ford**

The Personal Style Advantage

Knowledge about personal style preferences brings with it several important advantages. Here are just a few of them:

1. A model for changing differences into similarities

Personal style preferences are normal and healthy, but we all need to know more about the ways we are alike and the ways we are different. We also need to understand how to use such knowledge to develop relationships at home, at school, and at work. A model can provide us with the structure we need for applying such knowledge. Personal style theory provides us with such a model in the form of a system for recognizing and talking about the similarities and differences among people.

2. Performance improvement

Frequently the biggest block between you and success is yourself. The more you can learn about yourself, the better your chances become of improving your performance, whether at work or at home. Sometimes different parts of your personality conflict with each other, leaving you feeling confused and unsure of how to make the right decision in a given situation. In certain situations your biggest strengths actually become weaknesses. Knowing what your personal style is can help you to cope effectively with such inner conflict and will assist you in keeping your strengths from tripping you up.

3. Learning how to transform your areas of natural weakness into strengths

People tend to develop areas of natural ability into strengths while ignoring areas of natural weakness. These weaker areas therefore stay undeveloped. By capitalizing on your knowledge of personal style, you can achieve more balance in your performance levels. Once you become aware of the natural strengths and weaknesses of your personal style pattern, you can produce a more effective plan of action for developing your areas of weakness. By converting these areas into strengths, you'll be increasing your opportunities for success at the same time.

4. Increased ability to improve relationships at work and at home

How you treat others is often directly related to how you treat yourself. As you improve your relationship with yourself, so will your relationships with others improve. Because more of your needs are satisfied through your own behavior rather than through the behavior of others, your dependency on others decreases, thus relieving the burden they might feel when interacting with you. The stress caused by that kind of burden is reduced. As a result, they want to spend more time around you, because they are comfortable being with someone who feels secure and with whom they can enjoy a mutually rewarding, and less stressful, relationship.

5. Learning to help others in a more useful manner

Once you understand your personal style, you will be able to distinguish other people's personal styles better. This will include knowing what is most important to them and what needs are strongest for them. By shifting your behavior to meet their needs, you will be helping them in a manner that is truly valuable to them. If you engage in this type of style-shifting consistently, you will become more socially effective; consequently, people will want to be with you more often.

6. Learning to lead people and manage problem situations more effectively

Although looking at situations from the perspective of personal style is not the only approach that can help you be effective with people, it is the one approach that is most overlooked or ignored. For example, applying personal style knowledge can provide you with an advantage in many areas of management. Taking your style and other people's styles into consideration when you are planning how to solve problems allows you to develop action plans that will better meet individual needs as well as company goals. This usually leads to an increased amount of cooperation toward your established goal.

What this Book Aims to Achieve

Why Aren't You More Like Me? was written to achieve several goals. Each goal was established to assist you in obtaining the personal style advantages just mentioned. Together these goals form a strategic plan that will help you obtain the maximum results at work and at home by using the personal style information presented in the book. Let's take a quick look at each goal, or step, in the plan.

1. To increase awareness of personal style in self and others

The first goal is to help you understand yourself and others in a new and wonderful way, to guide you to a point where you can comprehend why you do some of the things you do and say some of the things you say. I hope that as your understanding deepens you learn to accept yourself and others in a way that is profoundly different from anything you have experienced before. This understanding will also assist you in identifying specific areas of your personal style that you will want to develop more fully.

2. To improve self-control over personal style

The second goal is to help you become less self-centered. The title of this book, obviously a tongue-in-cheek question, reflects that element in all of us which thinks others would really be better off if they were more like us. Each one of us in some way thinks we own the market when it comes to knowing how reality should be. Unfortunately, this type of projection and self-centeredness rarely leads to productive relationships. More often than not, it provokes arguments over who is right or wrong. This type of argument leads to struggles over who should have power and control in the relationship. By not allowing our personal styles to control us, we can greatly improve our relationships with others.

3. To expand personal credibility

Another important goal of this book is to help you develop your credibility with others at work and at home. Credibility is essential for developing deeper relationships that will last over time. How credible you are with others will determine how much they will believe you, cooperate with you, support you, and share their thoughts, feelings, and concerns with you. Like respect, credibility cannot be expected or demanded; it must be earned.

4. To transfer knowledge into skills

Knowledge is important, but skills make the difference. *Why Aren't You More Like Me?* was written to provide you with both the knowledge of your personal style and the key skills for appropriately using that knowledge. The only way you can truly improve your personal and work relationships is to increase your people skills.

People-skill development takes practice and, more importantly, a willingness to work hard to improve the behavior. In this book I will introduce you to three skills for developing relationships using personal style information: translating, suspending, and style-shifting. Like learning to apply any other people skills, learning personal style skills is not always easy, but in time it can be very rewarding.

5.   To enhance leadership abilities at work and at home
The information in this book can help you develop your abilities to lead others. It will provide you with some new leadership tools for your existing leadership tool kit. Developing your leadership focus and skills can greatly improve your results as a manager or a parent. It will definitely increase your chances of having a positive impact upon those whom you wish to lead.

Leadership implies going ahead of others for the purpose of guiding them to somewhere new. To lead others successfully requires a willingness on their part to follow whoever the leader is. If you as the leader cannot convince others to follow in the direction you are going, are you really a leader? Too often managers and parents assume they are leaders just because they fill certain roles within the organization or family. As a result, when they attempt to get their employees or children to follow them in a certain direction, there is resistance and often refusal. The knowledge and skills in my book can assist you to increase the willingness of others to follow your lead.

The Ultimate Goal

The primary reason I wrote this book is simply that I care about you and the people you interact with every day. Learning about my own personal style proved to be an extremely valuable experience for me. The knowledge not only helped me understand how my preferred style of behavior was working both for and against me but, even more importantly, provided me with quick insight into how I could learn to be more effective in my personal and professional relationships with others.

Such discernment has changed the way I think about and approach other people; instead of treating them as if they were like me, I now realize that what I want and prefer is often quite different from what they are needing and expecting. Learning about personal style has taught me how to assist others in such a way that they feel understood and are glad I am there for helping them. It has helped me become more of a blessing to others than a burden. I hope you benefit from it as much as I have.

Chapter 2.
Credibility Is Required to Lead With Style

You can make more friends in two months by becoming interested in other people than you can in two years by trying to get other people interested in you.

— Dale Carnegie

Dale Carnegie could very easily have been talking about developing credibility rather than friendship when he shared this great insight. His statement very clearly illustrates just how important meeting other people's needs are if you want to have credibility with them. The level of respect people have for us is directly related to how we interact with them. Our style of approach toward others greatly determines their perceptions of us.

Credibility is an elusive quality because our level of credibility always exists in other people's minds; it is a part of their thinking, not ours. While we can influence what others think of us, we can never control their thoughts, nor they ours. Our only hope of making a positive impression lies in how we behave when we are around them.

While we judge our credibility levels more by our intentions, others judge us almost totally by our actions. It is our behavior, what we actually do and don't do, that builds credibility with people, not what we had hoped to do. Our intentions and especially our verbal messages are valid only if they consistently match our behavior, and if our behavior also demonstrates respect toward others. Caring and treating others in a thoughtful manner is what influences the way people think about us.

Credibility is associated more with respect than with reputation. We sometimes get the two mixed up. You may have a particular idea about yourself, but that doesn't necessarily mean that other poeple have the same idea about you. For instance, while the school bully may have a big reputation on campus, he does not have any credibility with the students. He isn't liked, trusted, admired, or befriended. He may control situations and events, but he is lonely and will be deserted as soon as the students figure out how to get away from him. His very own actions destroy his credibility with the people he wants to have follow him. All too often the same results occur for leaders at work and at home.

Your success at developing credibility in different environments can vary from situation to situation. Your level of credibility may be very good at home, but at work it could be quite different. For instance, you may have many struggles as a teacher, a police officer, or an executive but get along really well within the family unit. Or just the opposite may occur: you may be highly esteemed at work but having problems at home. The same could hold true for your levels of credibility as a neighbor, board member, church member, and so forth, in the many other roles we play in life. Some may be high while others are low. The bottom line is that each one of us has to earn credibility by what we say and do.

Credibility is an important ingredient for developing leadership at home and at work. It is the foundation on which your trust level as a leader is built, and unless people trust you, they will not follow you or support your endeavors. Whether you are a leader at home or in the workplace, at school or in the community, there will be times when you will want others to do what you think they should do, what you believe is most important. While having a high level of credibility might not ensure that others will follow your lead, not being credible in other people's eyes will guarantee that others will not cooperate with you.

A Study on Leadership Credibility

A recent in-depth study on leadership credibility is outlined in James Kouzes and Barry Posner's book, *Credibility*. By doing extensive research with large groups of employees from several well-known organizations, the authors very clearly identified the attributes that employees think are essential for leaders to be credible. This extensive research reveals four predominant qualities for our consideration:

1. **Honesty**—Leader tells the truth, is behaviorally ethical.
2. **Foresight**—Leader sets and defines vision, provides direction.
3. **Ability to inspire**—Leader is dynamic, enthusiastic, positive, optimistic.
4. **Competence**—Leader is capable, effective, and gets things done.

While these four qualities headed the employees' list of what determines whether a leader is credible or not, there were other factors that employees mentioned as well: being supportive and fair-minded, showing courage, and being dependable. All of these characteristics are very important leadership qualities that must be demonstrated through day-to-day interactions with employees if credibility is to be developed and maintained. But there is still another way to increase your level of leadership credibility at work and at home.

Where the Tire Meets the Road

This book introduces a very unique approach to building leadership credibility by illustrating how understanding and using personal style preferences can help develop relationships. In our relationships credibility is where "the tire meets the road." Regardless of any special abilities that we may have, how we treat people always makes or breaks our credibility with them.

An individual's needs remain the same wherever he or she may be. We do not turn into different people when we leave home and enter the workplace, even though we often learn to act out different roles in these two environments. Underneath all of our previous socialization and training, we are still the same individuals, operating according to the powerful reality that works within all of us: our preferences for meeting our different needs. Understanding these needs preferences can assist every leader to develop an approach that fits the individual as well as the group.

By exploring personal style preferences, you will learn what these differences in needs are and how to approach each particular set of needs so that others feel understood and cared for. When your behavior as a leader meets the needs of others, your credibility level rises; people begin to perceive you as someone who isn't just driven by personal needs, with no consideration for others. The prospects of what can result from learning about personal style differences are exciting, but realizing them involves hard work and requires patience.

Hard Work and Patience Produce Results

I grew up in a small town located high in the mountains of Northern California, and having been raised "in town," I was considered a city kid. Just how "green around the ears" I was when it came to farming became especially evident when I started working on a farm one summer. I was 14 years old. I didn't understand the seasonal cycle of planning, clearing, planting, weeding, watering, and harvesting that every farmer has to live by, nor did I understand the perseverance required of farmworkers and the repetitious nature of their jobs. Consequently, by the end of my first week I had grown quite frustrated with having to start over and redo many of the jobs I thought I had finished. I wanted to see immediate and permanent results from my labor, but soon realized I had to change my attitude.

One of my many lessons that summer was learning patience. If there was anything that made me feel impatient when I was 14, it was other people telling me to be patient. Yet by the end of the summer I realized that most things in life don't come to us just because we want them to or because we think we deserve them; they come most often to people who plan for results and then work hard to get them. I soon realized that every chore had a purpose and that after much hard work and patience the results would be there.

Leadership is very similar to farming because there is a process cycle to follow if you want to develop a quality crop of relationships. Developing credibility and relationships at work and at home usually requires the same kind of patience and hard work that farmers need to be successful.

It also requires the right tools—and farmers are the first to tell you that the right tools make the job much easier. Personal style theory is one such of tool. When you learn to use it effectively, it will reduce the amount of effort needed to get the results you want in your relationships. With this in mind, let's take a closer look at the leadership process as it relates to credibility and personal style.

Chapter 3.
The Leadership Process

Goodwill is the one and only asset that competition cannot undersell nor destroy.
— **Marshall Field**

You Will Reap What You Sow

As sure as the sun will rise tomorrow, you will reap what you sow in your relationships. Building credibility with others follows this very old rule of common sense. A pattern of success is required for any human process to prosper, including leadership. The personal style knowledge and skills presented in this book will be most productive for nurturing relationships and building leadership credibility if you follow the process I have outlined in this chapter.

1. Always cultivate with compassion.

I always love to drive by the farmlands just after they have been plowed and disked. The soil is so well organized, arranged in rows that seem to go on forever. This scene reflects the obvious: a major portion of a farmer's time is spent in preparing the ground for planting. Cultivating relationships at work and at home is really no different: it takes time and effort to prepare people to enter a relationship with you.

One factor that can help speed along the process is compassion, which includes respect, politeness, and kindness. People respond quickly to others who care about their thoughts, needs, and concerns. Caring makes them feel valued and significant. If you do not show compassion when interacting with others, the seeds you attempt to plant with them will not germinate and grow.

Similar to a farmer adding fertilizers and other nutrients to the soil to speed up the growing process, you can add compassion to your relationships to speed up the process of developing credibility with others. Leading with style is built upon compassion for others and for oneself. Leadership credibility at work and at home call for it. Compassion is also essential for trust to survive and flourish within relationships.

2. Plant seeds of trust

Farmers realize that just planting any old crop will not do; they must choose one that will bring them the best returns for their efforts. They can't afford to put in long hours of hard work and spend all of their resources on something that won't last or that isn't going to produce the outcome they need and are expecting. As farmers get ready to plant, they must trust that the seeds they have selected will be the right ones.

Relationships require the same high level of confidence if they are to grow. People are very careful about whom they are willing to invest their time and energies in. If they believe they will get the return they are expecting, they will make the commitment; when they believe the opposite, they hesitate and hold back from becoming too involved. Effective leadership requires people's involvement. Without trust, leaders won't secure the commitment they need from their team or family members to lead them beyond the present and into the future.

Using personal style knowledge and skills can help you plant the seeds of trust you need to become a more effective leader. These skills will allow you to understand the needs and preferences of each individual in such a way that you can approach and interact with them more productively.

> *It is not the employer who pays the wages. Employers only handle the money. It is the customer who pays the wages.*
>
> **— Henry Ford**

3. Water with exceptional customer service.

It is no secret that the key to business and family success in the '90s is providing exceptional customer service. As water is the lifeblood of crops, this type of service is the lifeblood of any organization and family. Without it, an organization or family will not last very long. Many books have been written on business success and customer service, but we're still left asking a number of questions: What exactly makes customer service so important to families? Who are their customers? And why is one kind of customer service exceptional while another kind is just mediocre?

Family units are similar to organizations because they have set roles and responsibilities within the membership. Teamwork is important for family unity, and open and efficient communication is needed to complete successful personal transactions. As within organizations, problem solving and decision making must occur on a daily basis for the family to prosper as a team. The more effective the problem solving and decision making, the stronger the team or family unit will be. Many families break up or simply drift apart because thay were unable to cope sufficiently with problems and unable to make the "right" decisions.

Also, as in organizational development, customers play a big part in the success of the family. But who are these customers? And what do families produce and market to others? I would suggest that successful families are very interested in developing and promoting their reputations within the various groups in their own families and in the community. Again, the family's credibility with people whom they interact with daily can have a powerful effect upon each member of the family and the overall family unit.

Family customers would include members from other related family units, such as relatives and in-laws. They would also include other families in the neighborhood and the community that the family interacts with on a fairly regular basis. Other family customers may be found in local social organizations, such as churches, schools, workplaces, business locations, and recreational centers and organizations. Right or wrong, social success is often directly related to how others perceive us as individuals and as family units. The key to success is being sensitive to the perceptions of others without being controlled by them.

But what makes customer service within families and organizations exceptional? For me, exceptional customer service means that the internal customer service is as extraordinary as, if not more remarkable than, the external customer service. And this requires that both services exceed the expectations of the customers being served.

Serve your internal customers.

Who are internal customers? Why are they so important? Well, it's actually very simple to explain the answers to these two questions because these individuals are the people who are actual members of the organization and of the family. Be they employees, executives, volunteer workers, parents, or children, they are important because they are the "geese who lay the golden eggs." Production and service to external customers rests with them.

Can you imagine farming a very large piece of land without any helpers? Your ability to compete against farmers who raise the same crops as you but with many workers assisting them would be pretty limited. Now imagine you start out the harvest season with plenty of workers, but you never give them any water when they were hot or feed them when they are hungry; moreover, at the end of the week you pay them far less than what they expect to be paid.

It doesn't take a rocket scientist to realize that despite the number of workers you have, you're going to encounter problems because these workers are not going to work hard and produce like workers whose needs are being met. The same holds true for families. Children don't cooperate with parents who are unfair, and spouses often fight, rather than work together, when they feel uncared for.

Employee and family-member needs are the responsibility of leaders. Leaders who want their workers to produce "golden eggs" had better take good care of their "geese." But what if you not only met your workers needs but also exceeded their expectations? Nothing motivates us more to work hard and serve others well than being served ourselves by leaders who have compassion and high levels of credibility. Not only does it feel good, but it is also good modeling. As a roommate of mine once pointed out, "What goes around, comes around." We should treat others as we would like to be treated, as if they were extensions of us.

Stun your external customers.

Now imagine you have a happy crew who works very hard to harvest your crops because they feel cared for and treated justly by you. You set up your produce in a stand and put up big signs to attract buyers who need what you are selling. A crowd starts to gather around and look over your wares, but instead of buying, they get back in their cars and drive down the road to the next stand, where they load up with produce.

What happened? Why didn't they buy from you? Why did they buy from the other stand? These are good external customer questions. Every day millions of dollars are spent on surveying customers to find out what they will and won't buy, and what it is they want when they show up for service. Although very time-consuming, it is an absolutely essential part of business and family success.

The reality is, no exceptional external customer service means no profits. In his many books and videos, Tom Peters gives us many key insights into providing exceptional customer service. The concept of his that I like best is working on "stunning" the customer with your service. This implies that when they come into contact with your store, business, products, or family hospitality, they are immediately "knocked over" by how good the quality and service is.

Anything within the organization that hinders this type of customer service, both internally and externally, can be likened to weeds in the crops. If they are not dealt with early, they multiply at a fast rate, growing larger than most day-to-day problems within the organization and the family. Furthermore, as weeds suck the life out of plants, these types of customer problems can drain the energy right out of your organization and your family. Understanding personal style preferences will give you a unique understanding of how people can be so different and yet so alike. It will greatly increase your ability to meet your customer's and your family's needs.

4. Weed out what has to go.
Weeding is simply the process of eliminating anything that threatens success. In business or at home there are certain things that must be eliminated if growth is to occur. While many of these problems are situational, such as computer breakdowns or house fires, most of the time the "weeds" within our work and personal relationships originate from within us. They come from our own attitudes and characteristics. Just as we can have people skills that build relationships, we can also have destructive qualities that ravage them.

Ten of the worst kinds of energy-draining qualities people bring into their relationships include:

• Selfishness	• Dishonesty
• Bitterness	• Abuse of any kind
• Pride	• A critical spirit
• Fear	• Addictions
• Neglect	• Ridicule of others

Qualities like these should be, and can be, eliminated so that your relationship can flourish with ease. There is no other way to be successful. If you want your efforts to be fruitful, then you have to do the dirty work of keeping your behavior and relationships free of unwanted plants and pests. When you cultivate, plant, water, and weed consistently, then the harvest will be full. *Why Aren't You More Like Me?* contains many useful and constructive suggestions for this type of weeding.

5. Harvest quality in your relationships

I love to listen to good music. Whether a choral symphony or a spiritual hymn is being performed, when many people are singing and playing instruments that successfully fit together, I am always moved. The harmony of people working together to create something beautiful that others may enjoy and benefit from also impresses me immensely. This same type of harmony is possible at work and at home. It truly identifies and defines the quality levels within relationships.

A key part of leadership in the '90s involves orchestrating human efforts and abilities into team performances of genuinely high quality. Getting workers and family members who are different in many ways to be cooperative with one another is no easy task. It takes special people skills to be able to lead a performance that sometimes includes individuals who don't want to "sing from the same song sheet." Applying personal style "know-how" can help bring such performances together successfully.

Farmers are like conductors: they too must orchestrate many different variables if they are to get to harvest time. They must arrange for people and technology to blend together so that the crops are raised for gathering. Whether it is bringing projects at work to a close or raising children to reach adulthood, leaders must be able to synthesize using many different variables. It is a challenge, but one that, like farming, can bring a very rewarding harvest.

What will this harvest bring within your relationships at work and at home after all the hard work of cultivating, planting, watering, and weeding is completed? I believe that organizational and family leaders who have credibility and compassion will be able to reap a quality harvest in the areas of cooperation, communication, and creativity.

A prerequisite for team success is the ability of diverse groups of people to work well together. Their willingness and ability to cooperate with one another "make or break" the outcome of the team. These teams must be able to talk with one another so that understanding, agreement, and decisions are made. When communication is positive, creativity increases and people want to contribute new and more innovative ideas.

Creativity is the lifeblood of any problem solving, and leadership demands that problems be solved. Cooperating, communicating, and creating take so much energy and hard work that it is also necessary to introduce humor. People need to laugh and release the pressures of everyday living. Humor helps teams grow together in deeper ways and bonds team members so that they don't resent making the sacrifices required to start the growing cycle all over again.

Why Aren't You More Like Me? can help you harvest the quality you are seeking in your relationships at work and at home. Part Two will begin by looking at just what kind of people-farmer you already are and will end by challenging you to consider new ways of increasing your credibility with others. I hope that you enjoy the experience of learning to lead the way with style.

Management means, in the last analysis, the substitution of thought for brawn and muscle, of knowledge for folkways and superstition, and of cooperation for force. It means the substitution of responsibility for obedience to rank, and of authority of performance for the authority of rank.

— Peter Drucker

PART TWO

THE FUNDAMENTALS
OF PERSONAL STYLE

Chapter 4.
Who Are We Really?

It is surely true that no two people are ever exactly alike. It is equally true that in certain ways all people are the same. This seeming paradox is the vessel that contains the concept of personality.

— E. J. Phares

The Paradox of Personality

Consider the shape of a snowflake. Each snowflake crystal has its own unique characteristics. When examined under a microscope, the crystals reveal their own individual designs, where the arrangement of lines in one crystal is not exactly reproduced in any other crystal. The snowflakes look distinctly different; however, they also have a certain underlying similarity. They share a common geometry: each crystal is symmetrical. Its design is made up of a single pattern that is exactly repeated throughout the rest of the crystal. In one sense, therefore, every crystal looks different, but in another sense every crystal looks similar.

The same paradox exists with people. We are all separate, unique individuals, but we are also fundamentally like each other in many respects. Just as with snowflakes, while there may be an infinite variety of human "patterns" of experience, some sort of human commonality also seems to coexist. While each snowflake is wonderfully unique, all snowflakes are produced the same way, with enough shared characteristics to make them snowflakes. This is where the idea of a personal style comes in. Throughout our lives there does appear to be some underlying personality structure that influences how we make sense of the world around us. Each of us tends to behave in certain characteristic ways, or "patterns," when we are in certain situations, and we share those patterns with others.

Some people, for instance, enjoy being friendly to complete strangers. While waiting at a bus stop, they may engage other people in conversation by asking them simple questions or by offering unsolicited comments about the weather or the bus service. Their actions are often motivated by a desire to acknowledge the presence of fellow passengers and a willingness to include them in a shared experience. Other people, however, will wait quietly at a bus stop. They will prefer to pass the time daydreaming or lost in personal reflection. They don't see much point in sharing trivial small talk with complete strangers who are likely never to be seen again. Neither of these patterns of behavior is better or worse than the other—just different.

Of course, we can deliberately offset our natural preferences and learn to behave in ways that seem at odds with what comes naturally to us. In fact, we do this all the time. Learning, another dominant influence of personality, is a powerful force. It often overrides our "natural" preferences for behaving. For example, we may not normally have the patience for accurate record-keeping, but we can push ourselves to be better at it, especially if the motivation is strong enough.

Exceptions of this sort prove the rule, demonstrating that when we closely examine our patterns of everyday behavior, we recognize we do have certain preferred ways of doing things, and that these preferences are solid as rock within our personalities. They also underscore the importance of learning in the process of self-development. We'll look at this subject more closely later in the book.

A Bedrock of Preferences

Submerged under all the layers of our learned behavior, there seems a bedrock of personal preferences. This bedrock can be called our personal style. It is our innate predisposition to a preference for behaving in certain ways. It is reflected in our natural tendency to prefer, despite other influences, a particular manner of perceiving, approaching, and interacting with the environment around us. These preferences form the working definition of personal style that will be used throughout the book.

Chart 4.1—Definition of Personal Style
Personal style is your natural predisposition to • perceive • approach and • interact with the environment.

Personal style affects how we see any situation we are in and that facts we pay most attention to. It influences what plans and strategies we use. It can greatly determine what we want to achieve from a situation and what we will place most value on afterwards.

Don't fall into the mistake of thinking that your personal style is the same thing as your personality: It is not. The two are very much connected, but they aren't the same thing. In fact, your personal style is only one part of your overall personality. There are many other factors that have contributed to building the person you are, ranging from your genetic inheritance to your sense of self-worth.

We'll explore the influence of these other factors later on. For now, it's important for you to recognize that personal style acts as a kind of underlying foundation upon which the other factors build. Like the subterranean hardpan that supports the strata of rocks and soils above it, personal style provides an inner support for the learning that occurs during life.

A Key for Understanding

Although personal style is merely one category of factors that determine the development of our personalities, this particular category has a surprisingly pervasive and enduring influence on our lives. In fact, it sways our personalities and behavioral choices from birth until death. But how can this be?

It is obvious that people who are in the same situation do not deal with the demands of the situation in the same way. Even though environmental circumstances may be identical for all involved, people often react totally different from one another. Examining the definition of personal style more closely provides us with a key for understanding this confusing yet fascinating human truth.

31

The term *natural predisposition* means that you are born with tendencies that form an unchanging part of your personality — a part that remains the same throughout your life. Historically it has been referred to as *temperament* and *personality type*. I call it *personal style*. Regardless of what you call it, this part of the personality dominates how you think, which in turn influences how you decide to behave, which in turn determines how you interact with others.

For example, it is clear that, from birth, children do not react to stimuli in the same way. Like adults at any age, children exhibit personal style differences because they cognitively process information differently. This can be explained by taking a closer look at three human processes: perception, approach, and interaction.

What we perceive comes as much from inside our heads as from the world outside.
— William Jones

First, we perceive what is going on around us by gathering and interpreting the information supplied by our senses. Perception is the interpretation of what we record through our senses. Each individual gives personal meaning to the information that enters the brain, thus making it subjective rather than objective data.

Using this biased data we make decisions on how to approach the environment. Approach includes both moving away from people and things in the environment and moving towards them. It also includes not doing anything, remaining in an observant position. While we are behaving in these different modes, we continue to record information and to perceive what that data personally means. As this happens, new decisions are made for how we will interact with the stimuli.

Finally, we interact with the environment. This occurs at the moment we actually stop observing the stimuli and become directly involved with it. Again, as interaction occurs, new information is recorded and distorted, and new perceptions are formed. The perceptions influence our approach, which in turn influences our interactions.

This cycle occurs subconsciously most of the time. This simply means that most people have no idea that these processes are occurring in their thinking, nor are they aware of how many times and how fast it occurs during any one hour in their lives. People for the most part are not "tuned in" to the fact that their personal style is controlling them far more than they may want it to. This happens especially when we are under pressure.

Thriving on the Pressures of Life

As indicated by our working definition of personal style, our natural preferences play a crucial role in specifying how we prefer to cope with the environment that surrounds us. Whether we are at home or at work, the environment contains four main pressures that we must deal with constantly: time, people, tasks, and situations.

1. Time

The first major pressure, time, is a persistent source of stress. We are only too aware that we only have a set amount of time in each day, week, and year. We can never speed time up or slow it down. We continually have to pick and choose what we will do (and will not do) with our limited supply of time.

This type of decision making can generate high levels of anxiety, especially when important matters are at stake. Just the daily task of commuting to work on time can take a terrible toll on our emotional health after a while. Even something like going on vacation, which is supposed to be a time of relaxation, can become a nightmare of time management when the car breaks down on the way to the airport or when travel connections are delayed or canceled.

2. People

Second, there is the pressure of other people. We are forced to learn how to live, work, and get along with all of the many different people we come into contact with throughout a lifetime. This creates stress and tension because we have to satisfy needs, wants, and values other than simply our own. This pressure begins when we are children, in our families of origin, and continues to affect us as we grow older, in other social situations such as school and the workplace. It doesn't stop when we get married and have our own families, our new in-laws, and children bringing with them new and often interesting challenges of their own.

Of course, interacting with people can also be very rewarding. If you are a parent, for instance, you probably have had many enjoyable moments with your children. Each child is special in his or her own way and can provide much love, joy, and contentment in your life. But children can also be hard to live with and difficult to understand, especially as they grow older.

Indeed, relationships with people can be both very draining and very rewarding at the same time. Effectively coping with the effects of daily interaction with other people requires strong people skills. Such skills provide us with the tools necessary to survive the strain of the lows in our relationships while also providing us with methods for maximizing the highs. Developing these kind of people skills is a lifelong job.

3. Tasks

This brings us to the third environmental pressure we must cope with in life: tasks. A major focus of human existence is spent on working to accomplish the different developmental tasks of life. The effort we make to accomplish these tasks is referred to as work. We must learn to work if we want to get anywhere in life. Without work we would not be able to get dressed, feed ourselves, build shelter from the weather, create new products for use, or even learn how to learn.

Tasks in daily living are never-ending. Many are repetitious and time-consuming; nevertheless, we must continue to do them. We often work hard on improving processes and systems for making our work more efficient. We create tools that can assist us with our tasks so that our work becomes easier and faster.

At one time, many of our tasks involved animals. In early civilization we hunted them for food, an activity so necessary for survival that in some ancient cultures it took on religious significance. Later we learned how to use them as "tools" for work, shifting the burden of our tasks to them whenever possible; thus was born the term *beasts of burden*. Then, in many cultures, animals came to be regarded as pets; they could provide people with entertainment and fun, as well as with a form of companionship. Today our "beasts of burden" are increasingly the products of high technology, which at times can relieve the pressure of our tasks, but at other times leave us longing for the days of the hunt.

4. Situations

The last environmental pressure results from situations we find ourselves in. Situations almost always consist of a combination of the previous three factors, involving time, people, and tasks. They constitute both the specific and general conditions of a person's life, which begins and ends in one cluster of situations or another. For example, we are each born on a certain date into a unique family environment, which generally includes a set of parents and relatives at a particular level of society, in a particular location on earth. In this regard, some of us are extremely fortunate, others less so. But we all have to learn to deal with whatever circumstances we are thrust into.

It is impossible to pass through life and not be tested by the many adverse circumstances that confront us. Some people have to deal with the tragedy of finding out in their mid-30's that they have contracted a life-threatening disease such as cancer or a life-debilitating illness such as multiple sclerosis. Others must learn how to handle the pain of divorce, job termination, or the death of a loved one. Sometimes a combination of adversities occur simultaneously in a person's life.

Events like these will affect people in different ways and for different reasons. There are many different factors in life whose influence has a bearing on our personalities and how we choose to cope with the four pressures of life mentioned above. Yet, regardless of the circumstance, it's your personal style that exerts perhaps the most considerable influence over how you handle these four central sources of pressure in your life. Each one of us has very strong preferences for how we juggle different time constraints, how we satisfy the demands of other people, how we accomplish daily tasks, and how we overcome life's difficulties. Together these preferences constitute our personal style.

A Lifetime Influence

Stated quite simply, personal style is that part of your personality which you are born with and which does not change over time. Somehow it is preset from birth and remains throughout a lifetime to provide every individual with a consistency of personality. If such a part of our personalities didn't exist, we would be totally different at the age of 20 than we were at the age of 10. Aside from maturity, we are remarkably similar in nature as time goes by.

Personal style is like an individual's physical identity in this respect. Although our faces and bodies undergo many changes over time, we retain basic physical characteristics throughout the different stages in our lives. There is a continunity of resemblance that links who we are at each and every age. The same holds true for our personalities. This oneness of personality is our personal style.

An indication of the persistent manifestation of personal style occurs when we meet someone again after a period of many years has elapsed. At class reunions, for instance, we can soon recognize something of the "person" we used to know—even though there may be many changes in appearance, health, financial status, or other outward differences that are immediately more noticeable. We are simultaneously amazed at how much and yet how little the person seems to have changed from the individual we once knew. They often feel the same towards us. Part of the excitement, and dread, of attending class reunions stems from our anticipation. Will we be able to recognize others? And more importantly, will they be able to distinguish us? The energy rises when we are all there and the truth hits everyone that no one has really changed all that much.

With a good heredity, nature deals you a fine hand at cards; and with a good environment, you learn to play the hand well.
— **Walter C. Alvarez, MD**

Is It Nature or Is It Nurture?

The debate rages on: Is personality a product of nature or nurture? Does it acquire its enormous versatility from heredity or through learning? While many theorists play the "either/or" game, I prefer to believe that the answer to the question is that both are equally true. The real investigation lies in how the two coexist within the personality and how they influence the brain and behavior.

Your personal style strongly affects everything you choose to do and how you choose to do it. Even though you may have learned how to demonstrate social behaviors unrelated to your personal style, it still has an impact on your decision making. It acts as a filtering system through which all of your learned behaviors must pass. Because of this it greatly influences many other styles of behavior that develop during your lifetime. More specifically, personal style can be said to be the foundation for your interpersonal, or social, style.

Your interpersonal style consists of all the characteristics and behaviors related to your personal style along with all of the socially learned behaviors you have acquired. Interpersonal style is different from personal style in that it is more open to the influence of social learning. These social styles are strong evidence that nurture does prevail in human development. They would include your style of parenting, style of working with others, style of learning, and style of teaching. Your management style and leadership style also fall into this category. The different ways that one person goes about helping another can even be grouped according to different styles of interpersonal behavior.

Still, all of these social styles will be influenced in some way by your having a naturally preferred manner of dealing with the type of environment you are in. Despite nurture's bombardment, nature refuses to go away. But how does personal style do this? How does it affect your behavior? To answer these questions, we must first look more closely at all the different pieces in the personality puzzle. In particular, let's examine in greater depth the important piece called personal style—the piece that is so often hidden from our awareness.

Chapter 5.
Pieces of the Personality Puzzle

Though our bodies may be bent by the years and our opinions changed by the times, there is a basic core of self—a personality—that remains basically unchanged.

— Z. Rubin

The Uniqueness of You

As the previous chapter's analogy between snowflakes and people suggested, you belong to a club with one member. Your personality is exclusive to you alone. No one else in the history of time has been or will be exactly as you are.

Other people would have to live your life exactly as you have lived it to turn out the same way that you have. They would need to possess from the moment of conception the same genes that determined, among other things, the color of your eyes, the shape of your ears, and the texture of your hair. They would have to be brought up under exactly the same conditions you experienced in childhood, play all the games you played, suffer all the falls you took, and learn all the lessons you learned. In fact, they would need to experience everything in precisely the same way that you did to produce anyone like a person with your unique hopes, fears, desires, values, and characteristics.

Even if reproducing all the different people, places, and events in your life were possible, we would still have trouble reproducing your personality. We would need to recreate the multitude of interactions that have occurred between you and these factors and decide which interactions and which factors have had the greatest impact on the development of who you are today.

It's extremely difficult to assess just how significant any one of these factors has been in creating your personality. How much weight can be given to any single factor? There's no simple answer, and the presence of so many factors makes it all that much more complex. This difficulty poses a futher problem for us, because one of the factors that has exercised—and continues to exercise—a significant influence over your personality is your personal style. Consequently, in order to explain the special influence of your personal style, we need to distinguish it from the roles that other key factors have played in your life. We need to look at all the different pieces that make up the personality puzzle.

Factors That Develop Personality

There are a multitude of pieces into which personality could be divided up. For convenience, let's group the various possible personality factors into six main categories. These categories are listed in Chart 5.1.

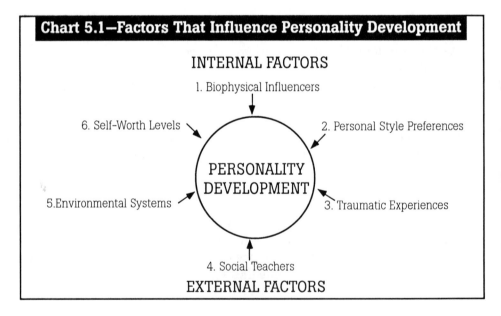

Chart 5.1—Factors That Influence Personality Development

INTERNAL FACTORS

1. Biophysical Influencers

6. Self-Worth Levels

2. Personal Style Preferences

PERSONALITY DEVELOPMENT

5. Environmental Systems

3. Traumatic Experiences

4. Social Teachers

EXTERNAL FACTORS

You'll notice that the three categories in the top half of the chart have been called *internal factors*. These categories contain factors that affect your personality "from within" because they emanate directly from inside your body or mind. Then there are three remaining categories in the bottom half, called *external factors*. These are more dependent upon factors that are stimulated by phenomena "from outside" yourself.

The categories have been numbered here according to the order in which they first play a part in our lives. The categories represent the different kinds of influences that are present to some extent in the lives of all human beings, regardless of gender, race, or culture. However, the strength of the influence coming from factors within each of the categories may vary greatly for each individual.

For example, everyone's life is strongly influenced by biophysical factors such as genetics, but not always in the same way or to the same extent. Persons born with physical disabilities, for instance, do not all possess the same kind of disability. And even when two individuals do share the same disability, this condition does not affect their lives equally. Some victims of thalidomide, the drug that produced a variety of severe birth defects in the early 1960s, have managed to triumph over their afflictions in remarkable ways. Others have not been so fortunate.

All this can sound a bit abstract, so let's try to focus on exactly what each category includes. We'll look at each category separately and examine the role played by the different factors within each category and how they influence personality development.

1. Biophysical influences

The first developmental factor, biophysical influences, includes any and all biological and physical influences on the personality and body that occur during a person's lifetime. Even before we are born, factors such as our genetic inheritance from our parents are at work in the womb determining a host of physical characteristics, like our gender, height, and skin color. Any and all biochemical changes that occur within the body (puberty, menopause, Alzheimer's disease, allergies) fall into this category.

Doctors, naturopaths, and psychiatrists focus most of their attention on the factors in this category. Biophysics is the "window" through which they tend to look at personality and behavior. They have strong evidence that the mind-body connection is one of the strongest links to understanding human behavior that exists. Take, for example, a very outgoing individual who loves to be with people and is generally the life of the party. He or she gets a flu bug and is terribly sick for three days. During this time period friends call with an invitation to come to a party, but the individual tells them "no way" and chooses to stay at home alone. Once the flu bug leaves this person's system, his or her personality and behavior go back to their outgoing nature.

This is a simple illustration of how something can effect our biosystem and in turn have a big impact on our personality and behavior. A more serious illustration of how biophysical influences have an impact on personality is found in the area of addictions. Here it is quite obvious that heavy and repeated alcohol and/or drug use can be very detrimental to personality and behavior, as well as to personal relationships and overall health.

Under this classification there are many other factors that influence personality and behavior such as:

- Genetics
- Sickness
- Birth defects
- Allergies
- Gender
- Body type
- Addictions
- Bodily malfunctions
- Stress-related illness
- Biochemical imbalances
- Health and wellness issues
- Physical and mental challenges

These sorts of factors are related to pressures coming from inside our bodies, even though the cause of a particular factor may have initially come from outside our bodies. Catching the flu, for example, starts when a virus enters the body. Once the flu germ is inside us, our personalities and behavior tend to alter temporarily to some extent. Even the most dynamic individual is likely to become irritable, to suffer fatigue, and to lack concentration.

2. Personal style preferences

The factors grouped under this heading represent certain naturally occurring preferences that people have for engaging with whatever environment they find themselves in. These preferences are evident in the personally unique ways that people consistently react to their surroundings, and are reflected in people's different needs, wants, and values.

The origin of these preferences is unclear, but recent scientific research is offering some clues. Based on conclusions drawn from studies of how various parts of the brain function, personal styles may be closely related to different types of information processing within the brain. It also appears that personal style—or temperament, as some people like to refer to it—is observable very early after birth, suggesting that our preferences are inborn rather than acquired through learning.

If indeed personal style is inborn, then most likely it is strongly related to biochemical functioning in the brain. Understanding more about the brain's biochemical development may reveal how personal styles are determined before birth. It should be noted, however, that the question of whether personal styles are inherited traits remains open; children often possess styles quite different from those of their parents, and siblings can have opposite styles. Furthermore, in considering this question, we must recognize that attempts to link personal style to birth order cannot easily account for certain discrepancies, such as why first-born children do not always fit the same patterns.

We do know children reveal a personal style that will remain unchanging throughout their lives; whatever style a person has at age two will still be evident at age 80, as it was throughout all the intervening years. We also know that each individual tends to process information (think) in a distinct way. This means that although people may record the same information, they interpret the information differently. These interpretations are called perceptions, and we have encountered them earlier in this book, where they figured into the definition of personal style.

As you may recall, the definition in Chart 4.1 stated that personal style is our natural predisposition to perceive, approach, and interact with the environment in a preferred way. All three personality processes are very interdependent. Our perceptions form the basis for how we develop approaches to the environment. If our perceptions are different, then our approaches will also be different. And if our approaches to the environment are different, then our interactions with the environment will not be the same. How perceptions influence our approach and our approach affects our interactions can be better illustrated with the following example.

Two people go to the movies together. They sit next to each other and watch the same movie at exactly the same time. One comes out of the theater, says the movie was great (perception) and returns the next night (approach) with several friends and enjoys it as much as he did the night before (interaction). The second person comes out of the theater, and says the movie was average (perception) and therefore doesn't go to see it again (approach) and doesn't tell anyone about it (interaction). "Different strokes for different folks" is an old expression that captures the reality of personal preferences and their impact on daily behavior patterns and personal relationships.

Earlier in this book I said "Personal style is that part of your personality that you are born with and which does not change over time." I also said that other parts of the personality do change through learning and experience. These two seemingly contradictory phenomena allow the personality to have both flexibility and stability throughout life. Let's consider a quick example of how these two opposing aspects coexist within us.

Let's suppose you attend your 20-year class reunion and you look around the room, and see Harvey. Now Harvey was the funniest guy in your class, not to mention the star player on the football team. But you hardly recognize Harvey. He's 40 pounds heavier, has lost most of the hair on his head, and has grown a full beard. You also find out that he has been married and divorced twice, has made a small fortune selling home-cleaning products, and is a gourmet chef. You just can't believe how much Harvey has changed.

You go over and start talking with Harvey, and within five minutes you realize there is something about Harvey that hasn't changed. There is that certain way of talking and being that makes you remember the two of you standing in the hallway 20 years ago. In spite of all the other changes, he's still the same old Harvey. The part that hasn't changed is called personal style, and it consists of all the personal style *preferences* you have within you.

3. Traumatic experiences

This category consists of any experience that has in some way caused us severe pain, whether emotional or physical. After a traumatic event shocks our systems we are never the same again. The memory of it penetrates beyond our reasoning into our subconscious and leaves us "different" from who we were before the event happened.

For instance, I had a traumatic experience when I was seven years old that still affects me today. Some friends of my parents invited our family over to go swimming in their pool. Although I did not know how to swim, I was excited over the invitation. I dreamed of how easy it would be to splash my arms in the water and propel myself around the pool. When I got there, reality set in, and I had to settle for clinging to the side of the pool. I crept along the edge, up to the rope that divided the deep end from the shallow end, and wished I could swim across to the other side like my 10-year-old brother.

Before long, my brother swam over to me and said he would take me across the pool on his back. I didn't trust him, but when he called me a "chicken," I took up the dare. Sure enough, halfway across the pool he dumped me off his back and into the water. He swam away, leaving me kicking and struggling for air. The water at this point was just over my head. Luckily, a man in the pool grabbed me and pulled me out of the pool.

This experience traumatized me to the point that I became very afraid of water. Experiences like this one usually leave us with some kind of an emotional scar, whether this takes the form of painful memories, hurt feelings, or negative reactions when we encounter similar experiences again. While I have since learned to swim, I am not a very good swimmer and hate swimming if there are too many people near me in the pool.

Traumatic experiences need not start out negatively, but they invariably end up leaving the person who experiences them feeling victimized. For example, a woman who gives birth to triplets may be overjoyed at first, but due to the extra amount of work involved with talking care of three infants rather than one, she might end up feeling quite resentful because she has no time to herself. While she loves each one of the children, the experience overall leaves her feeling traumatized.

Notice I said *might* end up feeling resentful. The same experience might not have the same effect on another individual. For instance, one person who has been in a very serious auto accident may be emotionally scarred for life, whereas another person may quickly get over the accident and still love to drive.

While some people go through life without having many of these kinds of experiences, and others go through life having had more than their fair share, we all have personal examples of such experiences. Even if two people have had very similar experiences, it doesn't mean that they were both traumatized. Different things scare different people in different ways.

The traumatic experience category is the "window" through which counselors and therapists often examine personal behavior. If you do have unfinished business from your past— for instance, fear or bitterness—perhaps talking to someone who is trained in helping people with these types of experiences would be beneficial for you. The main point is, after we have a traumatic experience our personalities and behavior change in some way; we do not remain the same. Are you aware of how you have been affected by your experiences?

Examples of recognizable traumatic experiences include:

- Divorce
- Physical attack
- Verbal abuse
- Sexual assault
- Road accidents
- Failed investments
- House fires
- Intimidation
- War experiences
- Natural catastrophes
- Job termination
- Death of a loved one
- Ill health
- Losing a limb
- Being rejected in love
- Seeing someone killed
- Public embarassment
- Attempting suicide

It is important to restate that some individuals may not be traumatized by events that are traumatic to other people. For example, seeing someone shot and watching them die may be so devastating to one person that it has a serious effect on his or her outlook on life, while the same event may have no lasting effect on another person. What might upset each one of us can vary for many different reasons, and developing increased sensitivity to the sufferings of others can be an important goal to strive for. Whether a person's experiences are positive or negative, don't judge their impact on the person by how those experiences might affect you.

4. Social teachers

Another personality development category consists of significant others whose personality and behavior we have copied. This social learning process is frequently called modeling. We use other people as role models and develop an understanding of which behaviors are desirable and which should be avoided. Frequently this learning occurs indirectly and often without our being aware of it. Much of how we behave on a daily basis is learned from watching and imitating other people's behavior.

I call those people we imitate the most, social teachers. A social teacher is anyone who has had a direct or indirect influence on how you currently perceive, approach, or interact with the environment. These influences could be either positive or negative. For instance, modeling has been shown to influence a broad range of behavior, from the aggressiveness of children to how children reward their own performances.

The social teacher category always includes the people who raised us from birth, in most cases our parents. It also includes other family members we frequently come into contact with, especially those who are older than us. It would include all of your peers while growing up and other significant individuals you have come into contact with during your life, such as teachers, pastors, and athletic coaches. Even media personalities, historical figures, authors, sports celebrities, and movie stars might be included in this category if they had a significant impact upon your thinking and behavior.

An example of a social teacher would be your first employer. My first employer taught me that while hard work comes first, there is always time for play if I am organized and motivated enough to get the job done quickly and correctly. She would say, "Slow down and do the job right the first time and you won't have to come back later and redo it." She also refused to pay me my allowance when I did the job wrong. If you haven't already guessed, my first employer was my Mom.

A list of social teachers who might have had some lasting impact upon your thinking, personality, and behavior would include:

• Parents	• In-Laws	• Girlfriends
• Brothers	• Schoolteachers	• Boyfriends
• Sisters	• Coaches	• Actors
• Grandparents	• Friends	• Rock Stars
• Aunts	• Peers	• Supervisors
• Uncles	• Neighbors	• Authors
• Cousins	• Religious leaders	• Artists

5. Environmental systems

This category includes any form of experiential stimulus we receive from the environment around us, a stimulus that does not specifically belong in any of the other categories. This includes all the general influences we experience in our lives as a result of our being members of certain social, cultural, and ethnic groups.

It also refers to any form of environmental stimulus other than the influence of people who have functioned in some way as significant role models for us. For instance, while a person's whole family unit would be included here, the role played by a specific relative would belong in the social teacher category.

We know that in addition to social teachers, we are strongly influenced by the environmental systems that surround us as we grow up. The first such system is our family of origin. This is the family unit in which you were raised from birth to young adulthood. If I were examining the social teacher category, I would be especially interested in how Mom and Dad treated me. In looking into the environmental systems category, I am more interested in how my personality was affected by my exposure to, as well as my observations of, my family's interactions.

Children are often the family's audience. Much of our childhood time is spent watching what is occurring within the family unit rather than actively participating in it. Within this category we are interested in information such as how your Mom and Dad communicated, problem-solved, argued, made up after an argument, showed affection, discussed sexual issues, and took vacations. Also important are other interactions within the family constellation such as how an older brother got along with Mom, a younger sister with Grandpa, or Dad with his in-laws. All these kinds of everyday family interactions created an environment that shaped our perceptions of and attitudes toward family life and, more importantly, life in general.

Other environmental systems would include any schools you have attended, the towns or cities you have lived in, the type of countryside where you grew up, the society and cultures that influenced you, military service, associations and organizations that you may have belonged to, even the climate conditions and acts of nature you have been exposed to, which also can have an impact on how you look at life.

Let's consider one example of how climate might influence someone. It is not a well-kept secret that in the winter many people suffer from seasonal affective disorder (SAD). They actually need exposure to sunlight for a certain length of time every day or they start to feel lethargic, moody, and depressed. Other people like sunlight but don't really need it to remain in a positive personality space. Some say the symptoms of SAD are due to vitamin deficiencies. Whatever the source, our personalities and behavior patterns can be affected by simply how much sunlight we get within any given period, and if someone is vulnerable to a lack of sunlight and lives in a cold climate, where winters are long, the influence of climate on personality and behavior can be profound.

The category of environmental systems would also include war. At any given time, there are on the average about 48 different armed conflicts going on in the world. Those who survive the experience of such conflicts are usually strongly affected by the violence and horrible social conditions they have seen. Often their personalities and behavior reveal major shifts as a result of exposure to war, which was evident in many of the soldiers who served active duty in Vietnam and the Middle East.

The following factors are some examples of environmental systems:

- Family of origin
- Step families
- Foster families
- Organizations
- Communities
- Religious groups
- Cultures
- School systems
- Places Of work
- Geographic settings
- Climatic conditions
- Natural catastrophes
- Cult groups
- Military service

6. Self-worth levels

Like the previous five categories, the last personality development category, self-worth levels, is an extremely powerful factor in personality development and behavior. It represents the different ways that our feelings of importance as individuals can play a role in determining aspects of the personality. Our sense of security is directly linked to our level of self-worth.

As self-worth goes up, so does our sense of trust that somehow we can cope with the environment. When it decreases, we lose confidence that we can be successful in our environment. For instance, it is not unusual for someone who has a high level of self-worth to overcome a negative environment and become successful while another person who has a lower level of self-worth fails within positive surroundings.

To get a clearer understanding of just how powerful this factor is, let's begin by defining the term *self-worth*.

> **Self-worth is defined as the overall value you place on your total being.**

Self-worth is a measurement of the deepest level of relationship you have with yourself. Every person has a relationship with the self. In fact, it is the most intimate relationship you will ever have with anyone over the course of your lifetime. It is your only relationship in which you spend 24 hours a day with the same person. It is also your only relationship in which you know everything a person is thinking and doing as he or she is thinking and doing it.

Self-worth is an extremely important personality factor because how your self-worth levels fluctuate will affect everything you say, think, feel, or do, both when you are alone and when you are with others. It colors your perceptions of your environment. If you have a high level of self-worth, then your perceptions will be colored by optimism; if your self-worth is low, then your outlook on life will be darkened by pessimism.

Note that self-worth is learned; *it does not exist at birth.* It is a product of nurture, not nature, and develops in us very early during childhood. It is also strongly affected during adolescence and adulthood as people and events react to our personalities and behavior.

To some extent, self-worth is developed by factors in all of the other categories previously mentioned. It is especially influenced by factors within the social teacher category. We come to behave toward ourselves in much the same manner that significant others have behaved toward us. For instance, if parents are persistently critical of small failings or imperfections in their children, as adults these children may have difficulty appreciating the skills and attributes they do in fact possess, but that were taken for granted or undervalued by their parents.

If reactions of significant others are positive toward who we are and what we do, then our self-worth levels begin to increase or get strengthen. If their reactions are negative, then we become weaker and our sense of value as a person decreases. This process of self-evaluation occurs within the mind of each individual throughout his or her lifetime. While the foundation for it is pretty well established by the time we are seven years old, self-worth development is also influenced by many other critical factors as we grow up.

The important point to remember is that our self-worth levels are learned, and whatever has been learned can be unlearned. The key is in understanding how self-worth is structured within the personality and what can be done to shift it from the negative toward the positive. Personal style theory can be a major advantage in this process.

Self-worth consists of two main components: *self-concept*, which comprises everything you think about yourself, and *self-esteem*, which includes all the emotions that you feel towards yourself. Humans have the ability to relate to the self from these two reference points. Self-worth is the combination of these two personal relationships with the self.

Your self-concept is based upon how you perceive yourself as an individual. It reflects who you think you are (your identity) and how you think you should act. Part of this thinking process includes what you "say" to yourself. This inner dialogue is sometimes called *self-talk*. Self-talk is directly related to the type of self-concept you have. Individuals with negative self-concepts tend to think and say negative things about themselves more often than individuals who have positive self-concepts.

For example, sometimes when we're driving down the street in too much of a rush, our inner voices tell us, "Slow down, you're driving too fast." When this happens the inner voice is said to be positive, or helpful. At other times when we do something incorrectly, our inner voices say, "Now that was really stupid. That was the dumbest thing you have done all week." When this type of devaluative talking occurs within our thinking, our inner voices are being negative.

Our inner voices in themselves are neither negative nor positive, but their programming—which includes the messages about ourselves that are stored in our brains—is definitely either positive or negative. Whereas the average person usually has some kind of balance between positive and negative self-messages, people with low self-worth always have a predominance of negative self-talk, and those with high self-worth, positive self-talk. How the inner voice is programmed is the real issue: What precisely is at work here, determining whether this programming will be positive or negative? Understanding this is a major step toward reprogramming the inner voice so that it is helpful rather than destructive.

Self-esteem is the respect you have for who you are as an individual. It's based on your overall feelings about yourself—your emotional reaction to the experience of being the kind of person you are—and reflects how much you like and accept yourself. Because self-esteem is a controlling factor in how well you take care of yourself, when your self-esteem level is consistently low or drops from a healthy level, others often notice. Many of us at one time or another have been told by someone who cares about us, "You should start treating yourself better," or have offered the same advice to someone else. Falling short of your values or abilities can precipitate such a drop; conversely, matching or exceeding them can boost self-esteem. The value we place on ourselves, or self-worth, can be either challenged, secured, or enhanced by this important component.

When major disappointments occur in life, we're forced to make profound decisions, doing so even if unaware that we're choosing to think and act one way rather than another. The most basic decision we must make is whether to continue living despite the difficulties ahead: Is life worth all the pain and hardship? Our personal degree of *willingness* to give the future a chance and to meet the challenge of our disappointments is instrumental not only in how we choose to answer this question, but also in how we choose to act on the challenge presented to us.

Your self-concept and self-esteem, that is, your self-worth, are directly related your willingness to participate in life despite its hardships. In fact, your level of self-worth is a direct measure of your willingness to try again after experiencing failure—of your overall desire to engage in life. It influences your ability to cooperate with others and your belief in self-improvement, and determines the amount of faith you have in yourself that you can be a successful person whom others truly care about. In reflecting your overall sense of value as person, self-worth establishes the most intimate level you can reach in your relationship with your "self."

One Final Caution

In theory, no single personality development category is more important than another in determining personality and behavior; in real life, any category can override or dominate any or all of the other categories at any given time or in any given situation. When one category is dominates the others, the others never disappear or go away. They are still there and can be used to assist a person in increasing his or her current level of self-management.

Worth stressing here is that attitudes and behaviors are socially learned and reinforced; therefore, all the behaviors, attitudes, and beliefs we have can potentially be relearned if we are not satisfied with them. If you would like to receive more information about your level of self-worth and how to learn to develop a more positive sense of yourself, obtaining a copy of the *Self-Worth Inventory** will help you.

* For more information on the *Self-Worth Inventory*, and other PSI-related materials discussed in this book, please contact Consulting Resource Group, 200 West 3rd Street, Sumas, WA, 98295; (604) 852-0566.

PART THREE

HOW PERSONAL STYLE AFFECTS YOU

Chapter 6.
Moving to Different Styles of Music

There is something about each person, a pervasive style that applies to almost everything he does. . . .
Probably it is not just one isolated behavior here or there that gives us an impression but rather a composite of behaviors that are indicative of a certain style.

— Albert Mehrabian

The Same Notes Make Different Music

If you spin the dial of a radio, you'll easily notice how many different kinds of music there are, each with its own distinctive pattern. We identify these patterns by using names such as pop, rock, jazz, country, and classical. Each particular style of music uses the same basic collection of musical notes, but each varies the arrangement of these notes to create different melodies, harmonies, and rhythms. This creates very distinct styles of music.

The same holds true for the different personal styles people have. Everyone has a personal style pattern. Individual patterns can be described by using four basic personal style dimensions, which correspond to the four primary areas of human interaction: *behavioral, cognitive, interpersonal,* and *affective.* No personal style consists of just one dimension, but some variation of all four. Like different pieces of music composed of the same notes, we are different compositions of the same personal style dimensions. And as the arrangement and duration of notes in a piece create a certain style of music, the various intensities (or degrees) of personal style dimensions in an individual create a certain personal style pattern. There are 21 personal style patterns, each with its own defining characteristics.

The relationship between the intensities of personal style dimensions and personal style patterns may seem confusing at first, and you may wonder how it is possible to distinguish between so many personal style patterns, but again, consider the analogy of music. Once you understand the basic differences between musical styles—the defining characteristics that give each style its unique "personality"— when you hear a piece of music, it's easy to identify which major division the piece falls into. You immediately recognize that jazz is jazz and classical is classical. The variations of intensity within the four dimensions correlate to the characteristics of musical styles. The more familiar we are with the basic differences between personal style patterns, the easier it becomes to identify them. (The 21 personal style patterns are briefly presented in the *Personal Style Indicator* and described more fully in the *PSI In-Depth Interpretations Booklet* (see note, page 53.)

Dancing to Different Beats

Our personalities have deeply ingrained motivations for why they prefer dancing to one kind of beat rather than another. These preferences, which infuse our style patterns, can be identified by using the four personal style dimensions mentioned above. Each of these four dimensions comprise a set of human characteristics, and each are instrumental in the development of the 21 personal style patterns.

Each dimension has a particular influence on how we behave as individuals, affecting the strengths of our tendencies or the degree of our personal needs in the following areas:

- **Behavioral**—the natural orientation toward *Action*
- **Cognitive**—the tendency to be *Analytical*
- **Interpersonal**—the desire for *Harmony*
- **Affective**—the need to *Influence*

Each of these dimensions is characterized by a combination of different perceptions, attitudes, energies, and behaviors.

To help illustrate how each of the dimensions influences human perceptions and actions, let's bring each dimension alive by giving it a human identity. From now on, we'll let the following four characters act as representatives for each of the personal style dimensions. Just keep in mind that although you are just like one of these four characters, you have all four dimensions within you, so you are somewhat like each character to a certain degree.

Bill Behavioral

Bill is typical of people who score very high in the behavioral dimension. Bill likes to set goals, to accomplish predetermined plans, and to be in control of what is going on around him. The behavioral dimension frequently motivates him to take on larger responsibilities, make quick decisions, and focus on future developments.

This dimension is the source of his preference for strategic thinking and action-oriented behavior. He prefers to work alone, for he has a strong tendency toward being independent. Physical energy is a main characteristic of Bill's style. He often performs activities which require hard work and endurance. Bill likes challenge and often prefers jobs or hobbies that require some risk-taking.

Connie Cognitive

Connie represents people with a very high score in the cognitive dimension. This dimension influences Connie's preference for analytical thinking and problem solving, as mental energy is a key characteristic of cognitive styles. Connie prefers to think rather than do. She tends to constantly question and judge whatever is going on around her.

This dimension influences Connie to evaluate critically any part of the environment around her, including people. She often appears outspoken or critical, and likes to give advice. The cognitive dimension motivates her to be organized and systematic when interacting in the environment. Connie has good perception and an ability to think deeply about things. She likes to interact with one person at a time rather than with a group of people. Connie is usually very verbal, but only when she is feeling confident about the situation she is in.

Isabella Interpersonal

Isabella's strong interpersonal score represents practical thinking and social harmony behaviors. This dimension motivates Isabella to care about others and helps her work in a consistent and reliable manner with others. She is a very good team player. Emotional energy is a significant characteristic of this dimension; it influences Isabella's sensitivity to what others think and say—sometimes overly so. She tends to put others before herself even when this causes her discomfort.

As Isabella is oriented toward caring for others, she prefers jobs where she can serve others. Non-assertive behaviors are primary characteristics of interpersonal styles such as Isabella's. For example, she has difficulty expressing her feelings or opinions in conflict situations. Even though Isabella puts others before herself, she tends to be very shy around people and prefers not to have group attention placed on her; she works best with others when the focus is not on her.

Andy Affective

Andy scores very high in the affective dimension. He is a creative thinker and therefore exhibits many expressive types of behavior. Creative energy characterizes affective types. This type of energy influences Andy's tendencies and abilities to express himself.

Andy represents the most social of the four character styles. He loves talking with people about anything and everything. Although he is very accepting of others, regardless of their different qualities or lifestyles, he likes his creative ideas and activities to have an influence on them. He will move away quickly from any source of negativity about these creative endeavors.

As an eternal optimist, a dreamer, he requires positive energy from those around him. When people or situations restrain the fulfillment of his needs, especially his need to be free from routine, he will bring his power of influence to bear on the problem, attempting to sway people's thoughts and feelings, or he will change his environment.

It should be noted that although I have used two male and two female characters here, the gender of any one of these characters could be switched without affecting the other contents of the illustration. "Bonnie" could be substituted for "Bill" and "Ira" for "Isabella." This doesn't mean that gender-related differences are insignificant. Such differences are factors in personal styles, as was mentioned in the discussion of biophysical influences in Chapter 5. It simply means that, despite gender influences, the personality characteristics are generally the same for men or women.

For example, those who are high in the behavioral dimension, regardless of their gender, are usually good at moving quickly in an environment. They tend to make quick decisions about how to proceed easily. Those who are in this dimension tend to experience more difficulty acting swiftly when adjusting to changes in an environment.

Chart 6.1 summarizes some of the main influences that the four different dimensions have upon our personalities. Remember that each one of us possesses all four dimensions to some extent. How strong each dimension is within us will determine how much it influences our actions and brings them in accordance with the dimensional characteristics shown.

Chart 6.1—Personal Style and the Environment				
	Behavioral	**Cognitive**	**Interpersonal**	**Affective**
Perception of the Environment	Environment belongs to them	Environment is complex, dangerous	Environment is big and overwhelming	Environment is one big adventure
Approach to the Environment	Direct, little/no hesitation	Slowly with caution	Slowly with trust	Immediate, impulsive, and fast
Interaction with the Environment	Takes charge quickly	Verbally questions or tells	Listens, moves ahead with others	Verbally influences others
Energy Displayed in the Environment	Physical action	Mental discussion	Emotional caring	Creative expression
Fear of the Environment	Low	High	Medium	Low
Will to Succeed in the Environment	Strongest	Strong	Weakest	Medium

Let's Do Lunch Sometime

Let's suppose that you, Bill, Connie, Isabella, and Andy all work for the same company. You and they have decided to go to lunch together but are having difficulty selecting a restaurant.

Connie doesn't care for just any kind of food and prefers a certain restaurant that happens to be expensive. Bill doesn't want to go to this restaurant because the service is slow and he has to be back at work exactly on time. When asked where she would like to go, Isabella says she can't make up her mind because all of the alternatives sound good. Andy likes all sorts of food, so he doesn't particularly care where you go to eat.

By the time the group returns from lunch, you're wondering if going was worth the trouble that went along with it—and the expense. At the end of the meal, Andy mentioned he had forgotten his money and needed to borrow enough from you to pay for his food. Connie then decided that the restaurant was not really as good as the one she had suggested.

Experiences such as this leave us wondering, What makes people react so differently to the same situation? Why is it often difficult to establish agreement on something as simple as where to eat lunch?

The inability to see things from another point of view is one of the major problems underlying communication breakdowns. We do not always behave in similar ways because we do not always perceive the environment in similar ways, yet there are many similarities in people's behavior patterns. How can this be?

One answer is that the four personal style dimensions are dependent on each other in such a way that the strengths of one dimension are actually another dimension's weaknesses. Areas of similarity between the dimensions are also points of difference between them. This sounds confusing until you see what the strengths and weakness are for each dimension. Chapter 7 will provide you will a visual aid in seeing these similarities and differences.

Chapter 7.
Looking for Similarities, Finding Differences

All the problems of the world could be settled easily if people were only willing to think. The trouble is that people often resort to all sorts of devices in order not to think, because thinking is such hard work.

— Thomas J. Watson

All It Takes Is a System

When I deliver seminars on personal style preferences I often hear comments and questions that have a similar theme: how to apply the theory of personal style to others. People tell me that while the information about personal style fits them well, they wonder how they can use it to determine someone else's personal style pattern. It all seems so confusing and complex to them that they don't know where to start, and if possible, they would like to use the information without having to think too much about it.

What I tell them is that identifying other people's style patterns is not that difficult if you have some sort of system for doing so. Such a system would allow for comparisons of some of the main identifying characteristics for each of the dimensions. And if they had a picture of the differences between the personal style preferences, it would even be simpler. They usually agree and ask me if such a system and picture exist. It is then that I present the Personal Style Model (see the following page, Chart 7.1).

Chart 7.1—The Personal Style Model

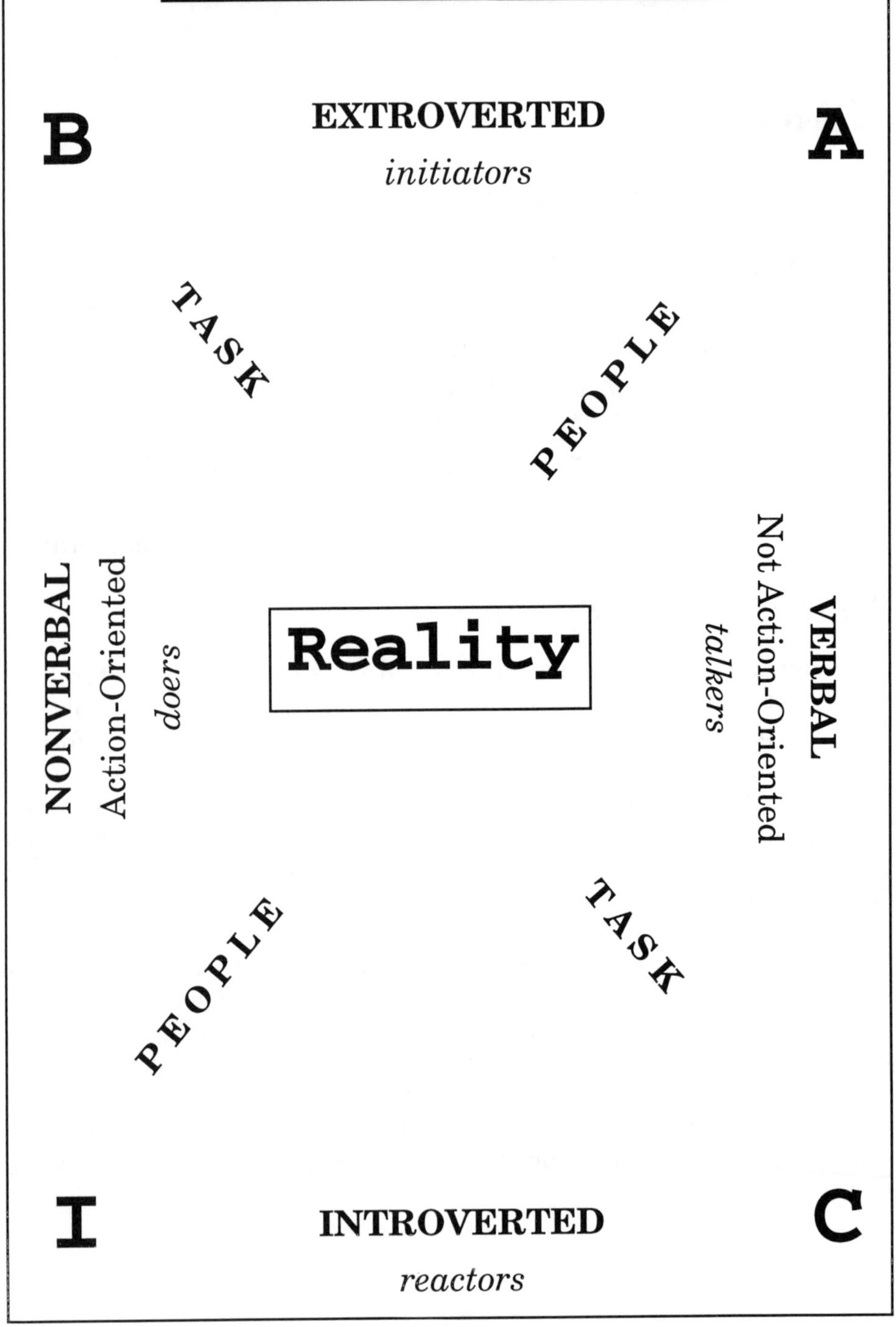

B

EXTROVERTED

initiators

A

TASK

PEOPLE

NONVERBAL

Action-Oriented

doers

Reality

VERBAL

Not Action-Oriented

talkers

PEOPLE

TASK

I

INTROVERTED

reactors

C

The model is simply a picture of ideas that illustrate how the four personal style dimensions are interrelated. Using diagrams to represent the relationships between the dimensions will help explain more clearly how each dimension influences behavior. It also provides you with a "system" for assessing others. Please refer to the picture so the "system" will make sense as you read about it (application of the model will be discussed in Part Four).

A Picture Is Worth a Thousand Words

The four corners of the Personal Style Model emphasize the equality of the four dimensions. In other words, no one dimension is more important than any other. The corners also illustrate the idea that each one of the four dimensions is distinctly unique. It is in each dimension's uniqueness that we will find both the commonalities and the differences between the four dimensions.

To measure and discuss each dimension's important contribution to the overall structure of our personalities, we need several "yardsticks" for measuring and labeling. The three yardsticks we are going to use each represent a different personality continuum. Each continuum contains two criteria, one at each end of the yardstick. The model has been developed using three orientations:

> **Continuum One—Extroversion/Introversion**
> **Continuum Two—Nonverbal/Verbal**
> **Continuum Three—Task-Oriented/People-Oriented**

Let's examine each continuum separately to see how they were used to develop the model and why each style dimension tends to influence people the way it does.

Continuum One—Extroversion/Introversion

Extroversion

First, if you will notice at the top of the model, what the behavioral dimension and the affective dimension have in common is that they both influence a person who is an *extrovert*. This means that if you have strong scores (40 or higher) in either one or both of these dimensions, a part of your personality is strongly extroverted.

> For our purposes, *extroversion* can be defined as *being biologically less sensitive to environmental stimuli.*

Extroverts are biologically programmed to respond to stronger, rather than weaker, stimuli. They need strong stimuli for something from within the environment to gain and hold their attention and to motivate them toward action. When environmental stimuli is weak, it does not hold their attention because they lack the biological sensitivity to appreciate (value) it.

This means that Bill and Andy have little or no fear of the environment and like to initiate action in the environment. They do not wait for things to happen to them but go out and initiate what they want to have happen. Often their attitude is that the environment is for their use. Even as children they didn't wait to be given a toy if they could go into a play area and take whatever interested them. By adding your B and A scores together, you can obtain your extroversion score.

> Your Behavioral Score plus Your Affective Score
> Equals _____ Your Extroversion Score.

Extroversion Differences

What makes this model useful and so much fun is that we can see the differences between the dimensions. We just identified the similarities for extroversion/introversion, so now let's go back and look at how the dimensions are on opposite sides of this continuum.

Even though both the A and the B dimensions influence an extroverted person, they do so in opposite ways. The affective dimension sways someone towards being socially oriented. That is one reason why A's are very outgoing, funny, like to entertain, and love crowds of people. A's are also very accepting of others and make friends easily.

The influence of the B dimension results in a form of task-oriented extroversion. B's prefer to be alone because they can get more work done. B types are hardworking and goal-oriented people who want results quickly. They value time highly and have no use for people who waste it.

Both these dimensions influence people who see the environment as opportunity. If you score high on both dimensions, then you are extroverted in both ways and regard both people and tasks as a source of opportunity.

Introversion

If you look at the bottom of Chart 7.1, you will notice that the interpersonal and cognitive dimensions are linked by their influence on a person who thinks and behaves as an *introvert*. Having strong scores in these two dimensions (40 or higher) means that your perceptions, thoughts, and actions are colored by introversion.

> Our definition of **introversion** is **being biologically more sensitive to environmental stimuli.**

Unlike extroverts, introverts are very sensitive to environmental stimuli and react more quickly to the subtle elements in their surroundings. In fact, they prefer weak stimuli to strong stimuli, which often overwhelms their "sensing levels." Introverts will choose a tranquil environment over an active one.

Isabella and Connie tend to be more discriminating of the environment because of their higher levels of sensitivity; therefore, they are more likely to wait for an event to happen, and then react, than to initiate an event. They perceive the environment as potentially threatening and prefer to proceed with caution.

> Your Interpersonal Score plus Your Cognitive Score
> Equals _____ Your Introversion Score.

Introversion Differences

On the other end of this continuum, we have the I's and the C's. While both are introverted by nature, they are introverted in different directions. I's are socially introverted. This is easy to observe in that they are very shy individuals. Even though they may love being with people, they don't like being in front of groups or being stared at.

C's are more introverted when dealing with tasks than people. Having strong perfectionist tendencies, they prefer to work alone in situations where they have control over what they are doing. This does not mean these individuals are poor workers but that they approach work from an introverted task perspective. C's like to think about doing things, and they like to talk about doing things, but they don't like doing things. When it comes right down to it, they often hesitate or stall because they are afraid of failing or not getting it quite right. They prefer to figure out how something should be done and then tell someone else how to do it, rather than apply their knowledge by doing the task themselves.

67

Continuum Two—Nonverbal/Verbal

Nonverbal

Look again at the model, you will notice that what the B and I dimensions have in common is that both of these dimensions influence *nonverbal* and *action-oriented* behavior. This means that people who score high (40 and above) in either one or both areas will use fewer words to communicate; moreover, when under stress they will probably stop talking altogether.

Because they are action-oriented, they are also very consistent in finishing what they start. Bill and Isabella both like to "get the job done," and they have very high completion rates. Please note that *action-oriented* does not mean *activity-oriented*. A's, for example, are very active but have trouble completing what they start. One reason Bill and Isabella get things done is that they talk little while they work. By adding your B and I scores together you can determine your nonverbal score.

Your Behavioral Score plus Your Interpersonal Score Equals _____ Your Nonverbal Score.

Nonverbal Differences

B's and I's are both nonverbal, but B's are nonverbal when working on tasks, while I's are nonverbal when dealing with people. For instance, B's prefer to be doing tasks rather than talking about how they are going to do them. They give very few details when explaining what it is they want to accomplish, usually preferring to talk about the desired results rather than the process of accomplishment.

I's are excellent listeners because they prefer not to talk. When they do talk and express their opinions, it shifts the focus on them, and being shy, they would rather not be watched by others. I's also have a high need for harmony and believe that it is better to keep their mouths shut than to offend someone and possibly start a conflict.

Verbal

On the other side of the coin, we have the A's and C's, who are verbal but not action-oriented. These types often use language to express their ideas and feelings, and have more difficulty finishing projects. People who tend to procrastinate have strong C or A scores.

By adding your A and C scores together you can determine your verbal score.

> Your Affective Score plus Your Cognitive Score
> Equals _____ Your Verbal Score.

Verbal Differences

As mentioned above, A's and C's are very verbal—these are the talkers. Their attitude and approaches to talking differ, however, as does the kind of conversation they prefer. A's, for instance, talk to all kinds of people and want to talk about anything others want to talk about. They prefer optimistic themes over negative ones because they are eternal optimists. They always look for and find the "silver lining in the cloud." They love variety and have a high level of tolerance for people from different backgrounds and situations. They like to talk to these people so they can learn about new experiences they might try one day. A's tend to smile quite a bit when talking and are joke tellers who like to laugh at other people's jokes.

C's, on the other hand, prefer to talk one-on-one or to just a few people at a time. C's are very particular about whom they talk to, when they are going to talk, and where they will talk. They are very task-oriented and more serious in their discussions. This means that they like to argue, debate, inform, teach, describe, categorize, and organize while they are talking. They also are focused on how correct the information is. They like data and expert opinions, which they often use in their discussions. They are also much more likely to focus on negative topics or themes. Others actually perceive C's to be pessimists, while C's perceive themselves as being realists who are sounding a warning to others to pay attention or pay the price.

A's probably talk more in a week than C's because they talk with everyone they meet. C's seem to talk more, however, because when they talk they often dominate the conversation. If C's don't trust you, they will clam up and say nothing to you. A's often say inappropriate things because if they are having fun, they don't stop to think about whether saying something is right or wrong. C's are good at asking specific questions to get at the underlying information needed for completing tasks.

Continuum Three—Task-Oriented/People-Oriented

Task-Oriented

Every one of us has an orientation toward accomplishing tasks and relating to others, but we have varying levels of intensity in each of these two orientations. For example, Bill and Connie are more motivated to complete tasks than to be with people. This is often indicated by their long hours of involvement in work activities and lack of involvement with most people except those at home and work. Isabella and Andy, on the other hand, have opposite levels of intensity in their task orientations. They are less motivated to accomplish work, preferring to become involved with people.

The common line between the B and C dimensions is that both influence us to be *task-oriented*, that is, to place a higher value on work than on socializing. Individuals who are strongest in the B and C dimensions are task-oriented first and people-oriented second. This does not mean they do not value people, just that work comes first. If you are strong in the B and C dimensions—as Bill and Connie are—you are probably task-oriented. Determine your task-orientation score by adding your B and C scores together.

> Your Behavioral Score plus Your Cognitive Score
> Equals _____ Your Task-Oriented Score.

Task-Oriented Differences

B's and C's are the two task-oriented dimensions in the model. If you scored high on these two, then you are most likely driven to get the work done. B's are task-oriented from a production point of view. This means they have set goals for which they want to see results within a set period of time. To understand production you must comprehend the concept of setting clear and obtainable goals, know what the work objectives are, and determine how much time it will take to get the job done. B's are masters at this. They are very focused on obtaining authority, on being the boss of the project. B's don't like working under others, especially if others are slow and don't know what they are doing. B's make decisions and perform very well under pressure; they don't understand why others can't do what they can do as fast as they can do it.

70

C's are also task-oriented, but from a quality-control point of view. They want to slow things down, to double-check all work, to make sure the final product is the best. They are perfectionists in their work and very critical of how other people do things. Creating orderly and systematic ways of accomplishing work are their areas of expertise. C's experience high levels of stress if they have to work under pressure for long periods of time. They don't like short timelines for production and get bugged if people don't value their "there is a right way and a wrong way to do things" attitude. C's are often overly concerned about making mistakes, especially if the mistake affects what others think of them as workers.

While both Bill and Connie are task-oriented, they are very opposite in how they are task-oriented. Bill is results-oriented; he sets goals and accomplishes prearranged tasks that are related to larger projects that he is striving to accomplish. Connie, on the other hand, tends to be more oriented toward quality and spends extra time working on tasks to ensure they will be done correctly.

For the purpose of illustration, let's say that Bill and Connie become partners in a watchmaking company. Bill would most likely prefer to sell a thousand everyday-wear watches at ten dollars each, while Connie would prefer to sell ten high-quality watches at a thousand dollars each. Although both are task-oriented, one is much more production-oriented, while the other is oriented toward quality control and craftsmanship.

People-Oriented

The A and I dimensions are similar in that they both influence people to be *people-oriented,* that is, to place a higher value on people than on work. If you are strong in the A dimension, like Andy, or in the I dimension, like Isabella, or both, you tend to focus more on interactions with other people.Because you prefer people over tasks, you put the needs of others before any tasks that you must complete.

To determine your people-oriented score, just add your A and I scores together.

Your Affective Score plus Your Interpersonal Score
Equals _____ Your People-Oriented Score.

People-Oriented Differences

While both I and A dimensions influence people-oriented individuals, I's and A's are opposites in how they approach people. A's are more self-oriented in their approach to others. While they are extremely friendly and accepting of others, they usually have some agenda and want to influence others to follow it. They are natural-born salespeople who love to talk a person into doing what they think will be best for that person. A's are very good at networking with others. They were born to talk on the telephone, and they spend as much time as needed to make their sale or to sway a person in the direction they want the person to go.

I's are also very people-oriented, but they are other-oriented in doing so. One of their greatest strengths, as well as greatest weaknesses, is that they put others before themselves. The positive side of this is that they are very good at supporting the efforts and hopes of others to achieve something. They are very thoughtful and caring, especially if others are in need. I's have the gift of compassion. They love to take care of people who can't take care of themselves. They often go into careers that allow them to work with children, the elderly, the disabled, and special needs people—those who are ill, dying, or suffering in some capacity.

Style Is Evident From the Beginning

As stated earlier in this book, personal style is that part of your personality which you are born with and which does not change over time. Remember that the definition of personal style states that it is our natural predisposition to perceive, approach, and interact with the environment in a preferred way, and that the environment includes the categories of time, people, tasks, and situations. This is why the three continuums used in the Personal Style Model are easily observable in young children.

For example, from birth extroverted children perceive the environment as an opportunity waiting to be capitalized on. Extroverted two-year-olds are strong-willed and quick to move into their surroundings. They believe they can keep anything they can get their hands on. Very likely to ignore boundaries and verbal commands, they can become resistive and rebellious when parents or others interfere with their plans for realizing success. These children are much less likely to ask for permission to do something and become upset when limitations are placed upon their freedom of choice and movement.

Introverted children, on the other hand, are much more likely to stay within the boundaries and to obey verbal commands or requests. They are very compliant with all kinds of social structure. These children perceive the environment as being very large and confusing, and accept social structure as an aid to success. They do not perceive things in the environment as theirs until they own them. They become quickly upset when there is a conflict and a lack of structure.

If you tell an introverted five-year-old to stay put in the living room while you go into the kitchen for a moment, that child will most likely stay put. He may get up and move a few feet, but when you return to the room he will go back to the spot at which you told him to stay. The extroverted child, in the same situation, will most likely leave the rooms while you are gone. She will either follow you into the kitchen or go into another room, perhaps even outside the house if so motivated. This child will stay in the room only if there are very strong stimuli to keep her there (other people, TV, and so forth).

The same holds true for the other two continuums. It is quite obvious whether a child is verbal or nonverbal, and whether a child is task-oriented or people-oriented. These characteristics are observable in a child's daily interactions and remain observable throughout that child's lifetime.

Benefiting from understanding personal style differences requires more than just realizing what the different personal style preferences are; it requires a working knowledge of why people are compatible in some situations and relationships but not in others. The degree to which we are compatible with others is greatly determined by how similarly we and they perceive the world. Let's now move on to Chapter 8 and take a more in-depth look at the subject of compatibility as it relates to personal styles.

Chapter 8.
Flexing Toward Style Compatibility

Life is more than a heartbeat, or the ability to breathe, eat, see and feel. An individual's life rotates around the quality of his relationships with other people.
Life is people, and it is not so much what they do for you as what you do for them and what you give each other.

— Maxwell Maltz

Making the Connection

Sometimes you can have a wonderful time at a party even though many of the guests are complete strangers to you. At other times, meeting new people can be a tremendous strain because you can't quite connect with their personalities, regardless of the effort you make. It's a struggle even to keep up a conversation with people whose views and values seem to be so different from yours. Indeed, at times you and another person may struggle through a conversation, finding it difficult to understand what each other is talking about. Eventually, you find yourself walking away and wondering why you both seem so incompatible.

What makes people get along well together? Why do some couples stay married their whole lives while others flounder through several unsuccessful attempts? Why do some people seem to fit in no matter what company they are with, whereas other people often offend and antagonize even their own friends and relatives?

There are, of course, a multitude of reasons why some people get along better than others, and most of these reasons are specific to the individuals themselves or the particular situations they find themselves in. Factors such as social awareness, communication skills, and a willingness to compromise with others all play an important part in how individuals are perceived and how readily they are accepted.

In general, people get along with others because they respond to other people as individuals—they demonstrate in their words and deeds that other people are important and valuable. They make an effort to meet other people's needs as well as their own. They are prepared to try to make things work out. Responding well to different personal styles is an integral part of this process.

While there are countless reasons why people "rub one another the wrong way" and don't relate effectively with one another, there is an important yet often overlooked reason why people get along well together: they experience style compatibility. The way each individual prefers to perceive, approach, and interact with the environment is compatible with the other.

For example, Connie's job as a researcher for a large oil company suits her well because she is naturally interested in locating information and checking details; however, dealing with the public or other company employees away from her daily job responsibilities—something her personal style does not ordinarily prefer—could cause her problems, especially with others who do not clearly explain what they need or who want her to perform duties outside her area of expertise. She usually feels mismatched or incompatible with these types of individuals, for they are expecting her to behave in ways that make her feel uncomfortable. On the other hand, when they ask her detailed questions about her specific areas of research expertise she feels excited; because their preferences now fit hers, and thus are more compatible.

Obviously, Connie is likely to experience style compatibility with people who have cognitive style patterns similar to hers, yet she can also experience style compatibility with anyone, no matter what personal style they possess, by applying the knowledge she has gained about personal styles. All of us can create the conditions in which style compatibility becomes possible if we learn to adjust our preferred behavior to match other people's needs, values, and concerns. How we can accomplish this effectively will be discussed in later chapters.

Identifying Your Primary Pattern

To understand style compatibility better, you must first know what your primary style pattern is and whether you have a secondary pattern. Everyone has a primary personal style pattern, but not everyone has a secondary pattern. The primary pattern is identified by listing down, in the order of their strength, the dimensions that scored 40 points or higher on the PSI. For example, a person who has the following scores would have this corresponding pattern:

B.	45	
C.	30	A, B = primary pattern
I.	25	
A.	60	

Sometimes you may even have two primary patterns. For instance, if you have two dimensions that score within five points or less of each other, you could switch them, which would give you similar yet different patterns. If the scores are six points, or more as in the above example then the stronger dimension will always go first because it is more dominate. But if the scores are five points or less, as in the example below, then you would have two primary patterns.

B.	30	
C.	50	I, C = primary pattern (1)
I.	55	and
A.	25	C, I = primary pattern (2)

Once you have identified your primary dimensions (those scoring 40 and above), you will want to consider if you also have a secondary pattern or not.

Looking for Your Secondary Pattern

Not everyone has a secondary pattern. You only have a secondary pattern if you have dimensional scores that are 35, 36, 37, 38, or 39. The primary pattern used in the examples above do not have a secondary pattern because none of the dimensions score between 35 and 39. The example of scores listed below does have a secondary pattern. This is determined by adding the 35 through 39 score(s) to the primary pattern in the following way:

B.	45	
C.	38	A, B = primary pattern
I.	25	A, B, C = secondary pattern
A.	52	

Knowing the primary and secondary patterns of both ourselves and others is a good first step toward developing compatible interactions; however, to understand style compatability, we must take further steps. What actually makes people style compatible? How can you improve something that seems to occur mostly by chance? When exploring how to develop more effective relationships using the concept of personal style, we need to appreciate that style compatibility can be understood from two different points of view: internal style compatibility and external style compatibility.

Internal Style Compatibility

First, your personal style dimensions may or may not be compatible with each other, depending on how strong each one is. When your personal style dimensions are of equal strength, they will clash more often, causing inner conflict; thus, where people have scores of equal intensity for two or more of the dimensions, there exists the potential for style incompatibility *with yourself* to occur.

Clear examples of this are individuals who are equally strong in all four dimensions. Those who have scores of around 40 for each dimension are most at risk. These people tend to experience a much more difficult time controlling their dimensions since their energy naturally shifts between their dimensions so quickly. This occurs because each dimension is exerting an influence on the personality with the same amount of force, causing conflict.

For instance, when this type of person wants to behave in ways that are influenced by the cognitive dimension, the other three dimensions intervene and disrupt the process. Similarly, when this type of person wants to act out of the affective dimension, the other three dimensions again interfere, because they are equal in strength.

This strange "counterbalancing" between the four dimensions produces a very confusing feeling. Individuals whose dimensions are fairly even often feel torn inside when they decide to do something. They are experiencing "internal style incompatibility."

The positive side to this situation is that these types of individuals often find getting along with others easier than getting along with themselves! Because they have high scores in each of the four dimensions, they have enough strength in whatever areas other people are strong in

78

to understand how others prefer things to be. They can connect with a variety of people and situations more easily than individuals who are very high in only one or two of the style dimensions. They have enough intensity within each of the dimensions to relate to other people, regardless of what those people's style strengths are. This brings us to the other type of style compatibility.

External Style Compatibility

External compatibility means that an individual's personal style dimensions are in agreement with those of other people. When any one of your style dimensions matches up with someone else's, then you are in harmony with each other from a style point of view. This doesn't mean you will agree or be happy together, just that you tend to perceive, approach, and interact with the environment in similar ways. This can greatly increase your chance of developing agreement with a person.

There can be friction between any one of the dimensions in your style pattern and any one of the dimensions in someone else's pattern. This is often evident in arguments where the two people involved just don't have the same understanding of what is going on. Many times these differences in perception can be linked to differences in personal style patterns, and such style mismatches often lead to misunderstandings and conflict.

A good example would be that of a husband and wife who often quarrel over how to discipline their children. Let's say that Connie and Andy are married. Connie, being task-oriented, is more likely to be strict about how their children behave. Andy, being more people-focused, will probably be more tolerant and forgiving of the petty misdemeanors their children might commit. This style mismatch could lead to conflict in family settings such as the dinner table, where Connie and Andy are apt to diverge on how to instruct the children about table manners. A pattern of inconsistent parenting will develop and become worse over time as one parent ignores certain behavior the other parent finds worthy of discipline.

Knowing how to make their styles more compatible would help Connie and Andy develop a more consistent approach to reinforcing the family rules. It would assist each parent in better understanding the inner conflicts that occur when one of the children must be disciplined. They could then establish consequences for the children's behavior that would fit both of their styles as well as the children's patterns. For instance, if Andy understood how strongly Connie feels about proper table etiquette, he could avoid intentionally provoking the children to misbehave at the table because he thinks it's funny. Also, if Connie had a better understanding of Andy's need for humor and lightheartedness, she might not raise her voice so quickly when one of the children laughs out loud at him for making funny faces while they're eating.

Not overreacting to behavior that is strongly influenced by someone's particular style is important. It can improve, even save, existing relationships and open up the potential for new ones. When the personal style dimensions of two individuals clash in many areas, the individuals usually end up avoiding each other and have difficulty in situations where they must interact, such as at family gatherings or job-related meetings. When the conflicting dimensions allow a close relationship, such as a marital one, to develop, the individuals often find that certain situations underscore their differences; at these times they experience mutual feelings of antagonism and would prefer to be apart.

In either of these cases, personal style differences result in a similar, but often mistaken, perception: that the other person is behaving in a particular way "for spite"—to purposely cause problems. It is far more likely the other person is behaving that way for a "neutral" reason: that is how the person is. In the sense of personal style, we can take this statement one step further: *that is who the person is.* Regardless of the company or the companion, the person would probably react in the same way given the same situation.

To illustrate this, let's return to Connie and Andy's situation and their different approaches to parenting. Connie does not possess the parenting style she has because she wants to antagonize Andy; regardless of whom she is married to, she is going to prefer maternal behavior that corresponds to her cognitive dimension. Likewise, Andy will naturally demonstrate strong affective tendencies, no matter what personal style his partner has. It is when either spouse expects the other to act as he or she would as a parent that friction occurs.

This same truth applies to how a parent interacts with a child. If her child's style patterns are different, Connie cannot expect her children to think like a high C would, nor should Andy pressure any of his children to be like a high A when they are not high A's. These kinds of parental pressures and expectations often leave children feeling unloved, misunderstood, and angry.

The secret to having successful relationships lies in solving the problem of how to be both internally and externally style compatible. There are two main keys to being successfully style compatible: flexibility and self-control.

Internally, you must have control over your style dimensions and know how to be flexible in deciding which style dimension to shift into. Externally, you must demonstrate control and flexibility in ways that are socially appropriate, as determined by the other people involved.

Success also involves knowing how to behave in the ways that are most appropriate for the situation at hand. To achieve this sort of social propriety, you must be able to control your behavior to such a point that you can adjust to any person or circumstance as required. In other words, you must be *flexible* enough to handle whatever roadblocks you encounter along life's highway and must have sufficient *self-control*. Let's take a quick look at both of these requirements.

How Far Can You Stretch?

We all try to stretch our limits in an attempt to fit different circumstances. Like different-sized rubber bands, some of us stretch more easily than others. Some people have personal styles that naturally favor this sort of behavior. They find it easy to be flexible, to adapt their behavior to whatever environment they find themselves in. They are prepared to give a little in order to gain a little. This does not mean they will not defend themselves if threatened, nor does it mean they are too mild and meek to hold strong opinions or to show leadership in a crisis. It simply means they naturally find it easy to take other people's perceptions into consideration.

In contrast, other people have personal styles that do not evoke such inherent responsiveness. Their styles are more pronounced, more dramatic, and more direct. These people prefer to do things their way and are less willing to "give in." This does not necessarily mean they are stubborn or unsympathetic; such people can be extremely supportive and thoughtful of others when they choose to be. It only means they naturally prefer to remain the same rather than to "flex."

Each personal style pattern (the relationship of all four dimensions together) contains a certain amount of flexibility; however, each style pattern is quite different in how versatile it allows an individual to be. These differences in flexibility are related to the influence of the people-task continuum. Some people naturally tend to be more adaptable in their interactions with people, while others are more adaptable with tasks. What makes this possible is the degree of flexibility each individual has in relation to tasks and people. For instance, Andy has good flexibility with people because he is so strong in the affective dimension, whereas Bill, who is strong in the behavioral dimension, is more flexible when getting work accomplished than when interacting with people.

Your degree of flexibility is reflected in your PSI score. Referring to Chart 8.1, look at your four separate subscores, one for each personal style dimension. Any score above 50 indicates that the dimension has a dominating influence upon your style pattern. Scores above 40 indicate you are strong in that dimension. Scores between 30 and 40 occupy a kind of gray area where strength or weakness is balanced out. These dimensions tend to be moderate influences. Any score below 30 indicates that the dimension exerts a weak influence upon you.

Chart 8.1—Intensity of Influence

Subscore	Influence
20–30	Weak
30–40	Moderate
40–50	Strong
50–60	Very Strong

Most people tend to be strong in two dimensions (above 40) and weak in two (below 30). Some people, however, can score extremely high in just one of the dimensions. They tend to be more style inflexible, which means they spend most of their time operating out of the high-score dimension.

On the other hand, some individuals have three scores above 40 or are fairly even on all four scores. They are more style flexible; they have a natural ability to shift back and forth between their strongest dimensions. This type of shifting gives them the appearance of being flexible, for they can change more easily in various situations and with different kinds of people.

Such style flexibility is illustrated below, using Flexible Francine's personal style pattern. Flexible Francine's scores are provided with her graph. Notice that three of her dimensional scores are above 40 and one is below 40. (Remember that the scores for all four dimensions should total 160).

If you are like Inflexible Ira, who has a very strong score (40 or higher) in only one of the dimensions and low scores (40 or lower) in the other three, then you have style inflexibility. This means that your strongest dimension is so dominant in your personal style pattern that most of the time it overrides the other three dimensions. This style pattern is illustrated below, along with Ira's scores for each of the dimensions.

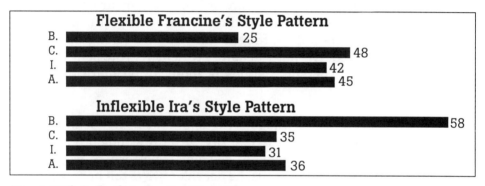

Flexible Francine's Style Pattern
- B. 25
- C. 48
- I. 42
- A. 45

Inflexible Ira's Style Pattern
- B. 58
- C. 35
- I. 31
- A. 36

But Which Style Is Best?

Neither pattern is better than the other. Whether your personal style pattern is flexible or inflexible, it is likely to have certain advantages and disadvantages. For example, Francine has a definite advantage over Ira because she naturally relates well with others who are strong in the dimensions she is strong in. Francine usually gets along well with people who are high in the cognitive, interpersonal, and affective dimensions. She also encounters few problems with people who have behavioral styles because her strong people orientation makes her accepting of them.

Ira tends to get along best with people who possess behavioral styles because he views the world in the same way as they do. Unfortunately, he also has to interact with others whose personal style patterns are very different from his. He most likely becomes more set in his strong behavioral-type pattern when around others who are different from him because their differences in style cause stress for him. Remember, that in stressful situations we tend to move toward our natural strengths and away from our weaker dimensions; thus Ira becomes more of a behavioral type, rather than less, when under stress.

A disadvantage for Francine, on the other hand, is that she finds it more difficult to control her behavior because she has to be aware of more than one dimension in any given situation. For instance, her strong interpersonal dimension could prevent her from sharing important feelings with her spouse when attempting to resolve an argument, because she wants interpersonal harmony. Furthermore, because Francine must keep three or more dimensions under control, she sometimes has difficulty reacting appropriately. In this area, Ira has an advantage: he only has to worry about controlling one dimension most of the time, and it is usually the same dimension.

Those individuals who, like Ira, have inflexible style patterns tend to have more difficulty shifting behavior because they are not as developed in three of the personal style dimensions. Ira's natural ability to appreciate how others with different dimensional strengths perceive things is more limited. His natural ability to demonstrate behaviors that are compatible with personal styles is likely to be more fixed than Francine's.

For example, as a boss who is style dominant in the behavioral dimension, Ira will be less likely to identify with the strong preference for details felt by his secretary who has a strong C pattern. Since strong B types hate wasting time on details, he doesn't always tell her everything she needs to know. His high need for independence tells him that she can figure it out on her own, without his assistance. Situational variables, such as other people or events, could shift you in or out of any one of the dimensions. Being aware of when this shifting occurs and knowing why it is occuring are of major importance if you want to take charge of your personal style and its influence over your interpersonal behavior.

The fact remains, though, that regardless of what your four scores are, no one personal style pattern is better than another. Each distribution of scores has strengths and weaknesses. A quick summary of the advantages and disadvantages of each type of style flexibility is provided in Chart 8.2, on page 85.

Taking Charge of Your Style

Consistent compatibility with others, many of whom will have personal styles that differ from yours, requires self-control as well as flexibility. You need to control the influence of each style dimension. Being

Chart 8.2—Style Flexibility

One High Pattern

Only one score above 40. This dimension dominates the other three dimensions and exerts the strongest influence on the personality. People with this type of pattern are very consistent in how they approach and interact with the environment. At work, home, or elsewhere, they behave much the same.

They do not have a high degree of flexibility when it comes to shifting out of their highest dimension. They tend to "live and die" with behavioral responses influenced by their dominant dimension. This tends to limit their ability to understand individuals who have different styles or who are style flexible between three or four style patterns.

Two High Patterns

Two scores 40 or higher. These two dimensions dominate the weaker two dimensions and have the strongest influence on the personality.

People with these types of patterns demonstrate flexibility between the two higher dimensions, but less often in their two lower dimensions. They are flexible between the two high dimensions, meaning that they can "shift" or move from one dimension to another quickly. Most people (around 60%) score high in two dimensions and low in two dimensions.

Three High Patterns

Three scores 40 or higher. These three dimensions dominate the fourth dimension and have the most influence on the personality.

People with these types of patterns have strong style flexibility because they "shift" between their three strongest dimensions quickly. They often demonstrate different, and sometimes even quite opposite patterns.

Four Even Scores

All four scores are very close to, or exactly at, the midline of 40. If the scores are not exactly 40-40-40-40, then they are very close to it. For example, 39-42-41-38 would fit this pattern.

People with this type of pattern have the greatest level of "natural" style flexibility because the intensity level in each of their dimensions is high enough to match anyone else's highest dimension; therefore, they can understand how others perceive things.

These individuals often get along with everyone but themselves. They tend to have strong internal conflict because no one dimension can dominate the others. When the B dimension suggests doing something, the other three dimensions respond, "No way!" Whenever the I dimension suggests something, the other three dimensions say, "You have got to be kidding!"

internally and externally compatible necessitates that you be in charge of your style pattern. This is important because you have a choice: either you control your style pattern or it will control you. When you are in control, you can better match styles of behavior to situational factors. In other words, you can choose to operate out of the dimension that best fits whatever forces are most dominant in any particular situation. To achieve this inner control of your style pattern, you need to take charge of how each dimension influences your behavior, regardless of the strength or weakness of the dimension.

A useful way to understand self-control of your style pattern is to think of the four dimensions as if they were children. If your style tends to be inflexible like Ira's (see the diagram below), then we could say that one of your children is quite a bit older than the other three. Just as the oldest child in a family is usually bigger and stronger than the younger siblings, so the stronger dimension will dominate the other three and demand more of your attention. In doing so, it will have a stronger influence on your decision making and behavior. People might say about you, "Yeah, he'll never change," or "She's the same no matter what the situation is."

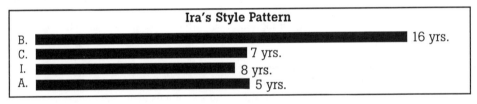

Ira's Style Pattern

B. 16 yrs.
C. 7 yrs.
I. 8 yrs.
A. 5 yrs.

On the other hand, if your style tends to be flexible like Francine's (see the pattern below), then more than one dimension is trying to influence you at the same time. This can provoke conflict between the strongest dimensions, for each demand your attention. In effect, each "child" is trying to influence you to do what best fits his or her preference. This type of inner conflict can often leave you wondering, Who am I really? You may find others saying to you, Will you make up your mind one way or the other, and stick to it?

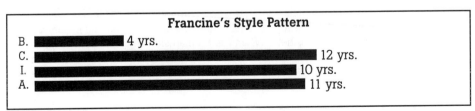

Francine's Style Pattern

B. 4 yrs.
C. 12 yrs.
I. 10 yrs.
A. 11 yrs.

Regardless of how flexible or inflexible your style pattern is, you still have four dimensions that can be either your best friends or your worst enemies. Much like parents who do not know how to control their children, people who do not know how to control their dimensions might very well experience extreme frustration. Taking charge of each of the four dimensions is the only way to unite into a team that works together for your common good.

The key question is, How do you control these four dimensions (children) in such a way that you can gain cooperation and teamwork? As a parent, you must meet each child's needs if you want to keep those needs satisfied. So it is with each one of the dimensions. Knowing what needs are associated with which dimensions—and being able to behave in such a way as to meet the needs of each dimension—will keep you in control of your style.

To achieve this type of self-control, you should let your behavior be guided by an appreciation of the following four key points:

1. Realize that you are stronger than your personal style pattern. While these dimensions make up a large part of your personality, they are not your entire personality. You can override your natural preferences. You can learn to take charge of each dimension to help yourself and others better.

2. Know how strong each dimension is. Learn to identify how each dimension works to influence your behavior, and learn to recognize what is special about each dimension.

3. Distinguish how your personal style pattern helps and hinders you in everyday situations. Know when you are being influenced by a particular dimension. Get to know your mood swings so you can appreciate how they may affect your behavior.

4. Make a conscious decision to take charge and then do so. Being in control is your choice. Do not allow your personal style dimensions to force you into behaving in ways that are inappropriate for the situation you are in.

How Well Do You Match Up?

Once you have a good understanding of your own level of flexibility and self-control, the focus can shift to how well your style pattern matches other people's patterns. Looking at how to improve personal relationships from the perspective of personal style theory can be fun as well as educational. Instead of getting frustrated with other people's behavior, you can actually become absorbed in trying to detect what their personal styles are. Later chapters in this book will explain how to do this in more detail. For now, if you compare your scores on the PSI with other people's scores, you will be able to see areas of potential agreement and disagreement between the style patterns

If you would like to compare your style pattern with someone else's pattern, start completing the PSI with that person. Then, using different colored ink, both of you should fill out the response sheet again, this time marking the descriptive terms according to how you perceive each other's behavior. Afterwards, compare your scores.

Areas of strongest compatibility will have close scores (within 10 points of each other). These areas can be called "overlap." The dimensions in which you overlap tend to be those in which you and the other person are most compatible. When you are both operating out of these dimensions, you and this person are more likely to agree or "see" things in the same way.

Next, look for areas of incompatibility. These will be reflected in the scores with the largest gaps between them. Let's call them "overgaps." The overgaps will reveal areas where you and the other person have the most incompatible behavior patterns. Possible conflict will occur in those dimensions in which the two scores are separated by a difference of more than 10 points.

For example, the graph below depicts the relationship between the married couple Bill and Isabella.

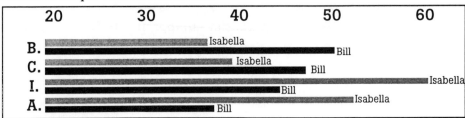

Their profiles suggest that potential areas for disagreement would be in the behavioral dimension, where there is a difference of 25 points, and in the affective dimension, where there is a spread of 20 points. The interpersonal and cognitive dimensions are probably compatible areas because the scores here are within 10 points of each other. Remember that scores above 40 tend to dominate the individual's personal style.

In this particular profile, Bill has high B-C scores, while Isabella is highest in the A-I dimensions. From these scores we could presume that Bill is predominantly task-oriented; he is extroverted when working, yet rather introverted socially. Isabella seems more people-focused than her husband. She most likely is an introvert in work situations and an extrovert when at social gatherings. Clearly there could be areas of conflict with this couple if they haven't already learned how to shift their respective behavior to meet each other's needs. Remember, regardless of gender, an individual could be any combination of the four style dimensions. For example, Bill could be the one strong in the people-orientation dimensions, with Isabella being more task-oriented.

Will We Get Along?

How well do people with different styles get along with each other? To answer this we must bear in mind that while every dimension has certain elements in common with each of the other dimensions, it also has elements that differ. For example, in the PSI model both the affective and behavioral dimensions influence people to be extroverted, yet some individuals are extroverted toward tasks (B), whereas the others are extroverted toward people (A). Even though in one way they are the same extroverts, in another way they are opposites (either verbal or nonverbal, either task- or people-oriented). This kind of relationship between dimensions can lead to many different and fascinating combinations.

The effect of style compatibility on human relationships cannot be completely explained by examining personal style differences. There are many other factors that influence how people relate to one another. A number of these factors were examined in Chapter 5. Nonetheless, some generalizations about how each style dimension affects a relationship can be made. If we were to examine compatibility between Connie and Isabella, for example, we would want to start with what is unique about each of them. Connie is task-oriented, introverted, and verbal. Isabella is people-oriented, introverted, and nonverbal. These two would probably work well together as co-workers because of Isabella's harmonious style of interacting with people.

They would also get along well socially as long as Connie was not verbally critical of Isabella. Isabella's natural tendency not to speak up for herself may irritate Connie, who prides herself on speaking her mind. Isabella's lack of assertiveness could also prompt Connie to attempt to control the relationship, thus causing stress for both of them. If indeed Connie and Isabella were co-workers and were not getting along well, knowledge of the underlying problem, however general, could be helpful to them, as well as to their boss and co-workers.

Further information on each possible combination of style dimensions and their influence on relationships has been condensed into a handy reference chart, which is presented in Chart 8.3 on page 91.

Chart 8.3—Personal Style Compatibility

The following chart is a brief overview of how individuals who are strong in a particular personal style dimension might interact with a person who is strong in another personal style dimension. The comments are presented as suggestions only.

B   Strong Behavioral Types and Other Strong Behavioral Types   B

AREAS OF COMPATIBILITY
B's respect one another. They like each other's decisiveness and action-orientation, and make good friends if both have similar interests. They work well under stress.

AREAS OF INCOMPATIBILITY
Conflict can occur between B's if both want to be in charge and have opposing values and goals. They can be aggressive enemies when they are in conflict situations.

C   Strong Cognitive Types and Strong Behavioral Types   B

AREAS OF COMPATIBILITY
C's and B's work well together if B is the boss and respects C's abilities and views. B's concern for production plus C's need for quality control can result in a mutually beneficial work relationship.

AREAS OF INCOMPATIBILITY
C's and B's might not make good friends because their interests can be very different and both need/want control. Conflict is likely if C is B's boss and C is blunt, indecisive, or incompetent.

B   Strong Behavioral Types and Strong Interpersonal Types   I

AREAS OF COMPATIBILITY
B's and I's make a good work team when B is in charge and I follows through with the tasks. B's will like I's loyalty, ability to help people, and ability to get tasks done on time. I's like B's fairness, hard work ethic, and ability to lead.

AREAS OF INCOMPATIBILITY
I's can be easily dominated by B's and hurt if B's are uncaring. B's need to be sensitive to I's need for appreciation, and I's can gain B's respect by being more direct and assertive.

A   Strong Affective Types and Strong Behavioral Types   B

AREAS OF COMPATIBILITY
A's and B's make very good team workers if B is tolerant of A's creative and people strengths. A lets B teach him/her how to increase production and manage time better.

AREAS OF INCOMPATIBILITY
B's may not like A's unreliability as well as inconsistent performance. A's may not like B's drive for results and low concern for other people's problems and feelings.

C   Strong Cognitive Types and Other Strong Cognitive Types   C

AREAS OF COMPATIBILITY
C's both enjoy deep talks and learning about self, people, and issues. They can be very loyal friends and good co-workers as both share similar values and opinions.

AREAS OF INCOMPATIBILITY
C's may have many verbal disagreements and avoid each other. They can both be critical of others, but neither accepts criticism well unless trust levels are high.

Chart 8.3—Continued

C — Strong Interpersonal Types and Strong Cognitive Types — I

AREAS OF COMPATIBILITY

C's and I's often work well together and get along socially due to I's need for harmony and C's need for intimacy. They are both family-oriented, fun loving, and honest. I's can help C's be tolerant of others and C's can help I's be assertive.

AREAS OF INCOMPATIBILITY

C's can be too blunt and critical of I's, leading to hurt feelings and resentment. C's may have trouble with I's not being assertive enough, while I's may have trouble with C's tendency to be critical.

A — Strong Cognitive Types and Strong Affective Types — C

AREAS OF COMPATIBILITY

There are few areas of compatibility between these two styles as they resemble the original "Odd Couple." If A's and C's understand each other's strengths and don't try to force one another to change, they can effectively work together.

AREAS OF INCOMPATIBILITY

A's may resent C's inflexible attitudes and behaviors. C's may be intolerant of A's lack of commitment and avoidance of work and responsibility. Conflict is likely between such opposite styles.

I — Strong Interpersonal Types and Other Strong Interpersonal Types — I

AREAS OF COMPATIBILITY

I's work and socalize well together, make good friends, and are reliable co-workers. They enjoy each other at work and at home, love to talk and do things together. They can make a good team for helping or parenting.

AREAS OF INCOMPATIBILITY

I's can have trouble with making big decisions or in working out disagreements. Stubbornness may cause frustration and avoidance. They may sometimes be untruthful to protect the other's feelings.

I — Strong Interpersonal Types and Strong Affective Types — A

AREAS OF COMPATIBILITY

I's and A's socialize very well. A's add fun to I's practical routine and stimulate I's creativity. I's can help A's to stay focused on tasks needing completion. They can make a good people-helping team.

AREAS OF INCOMPATIBILITY

A's may take advantage of I's caring and unselfishness. I's will feel stress if A's are financially or socially irresponsible. They may not be the best team for making big decisions carefully.

A — Strong Affective Types and Other Strong Affective Types — A

AREAS OF COMPATIBILITY

A's are very socially compatible as both enjoy activities, excitement, and variety. They are very people-oriented and like to have fun. A's can make a good sales or people-helping team when they stay on the task.

AREAS OF INCOMPATIBILITY

A's may not finish projects due to sociable nature and lack of concentration on tasks and time. Impulsive decision-making and spending could cause difficulties.

Chapter 9.
Different Motivational Preferences

By distinguishing types according to their own strivings and values, we are trying to develop knowledge that increases compassion, respect for differences but also understanding of what we like and dislike in ourselves and others and why. . . .

— Michael Maccoby

Driving Through Life

Our lives are like vehicles we steer through the greater dimensions—the vast roadways and intricate networks—of life itself. Many of us drive in similar directions, heading toward similar destinations; others choose to travel against the flow, with different destinations in mind. The locations at which we hope to arrive tell much about who we are and what is most important to us. How fast we drive also provides valuable insights into our nature and desires. Many people drive slowly and cautiously or refuse to drive at all because they're afraid of accidents; while others speed along recklessly, so afraid of not reaching a destination in time that they disregard the possibility of a mishap occurring. What compels each of us to be a particular type of driver? And why do we choose to head in different directions in life?

Some force seems at work within us, creating a state of tension that makes us move in a certain direction, in a certain way—to strive toward specific rewards or goals. It is the same force that trips a redlight when we veer off the road that is most true to our nature and head toward things we don't value. That force is called *motivation*: the impulse to behave in a particular way. As an inner power it compels us to move in one direction rather than another, redirecting us when new roadways offer better opportunies than the ones we're currently traveling on. Whether motivation pressures us to move forward, to redirect our lives, or to simply stop for the moment depends upon the many internal and external variables involved in our lives at any particular point in time. Some of the internal variables directly related to motivation are needs, fears, and values.

All of us are motived by different needs, fears, and values. What motivates me to behave in certain ways may not motivate you. For example, I've spend long hours sitting at a computer, writing this book. The decision to use this time to produce a book rather than to do something else was motivated by my needs, fears, and values. These variables may differ for you, inspiring you to use your time to complete tasks such as restoring an old car or learning a foreign language. The interesting question, therefore, is this: How are individuals inspired to do one thing rather than another? Understanding the answer to this question is a key to understanding other people and ourselves.

Inspiration, then, is the impulse which sets creation in movement; it is also the energy which keeps it going.

— Roger Sessions

Going to the Store

Before we go shopping, we often ask others if they need anything from the store. It is a sign of caring and respect for other people's needs. We realize that sometimes people cannot do what they need to do right away, and we are more than willing to help them if we can. If only we were as quick to take other people's personal needs into account on a more daily basis. Such consideration would improve our relationships with others, which in turn would help us get needs met also.

For example, Andy needs acceptance from others. By asking Isabella if she would like something from the store, he is showing that he cares enough to do something for her. If he follows through and brings home what she asked for, he is meeting her psychological needs as well as her physical needs. Such helpful actions speak loudly to Isabella. She, in turn, will be more than willing to show signs of acceptance for him, because she appreciates his thoughtfulness. When her needs are met, she becomes more motivated to meet his needs.

Theories of motivation suggest we are stimulated to move toward things that meet our predominant needs and to move away from activities that do not meet our needs. *When something consistently meets a particular need of ours, it becomes more attractive and valuable to us.* We value most whatever best meets our needs.

We can tell what is important to us by listening to the "voice" of our feelings. Feelings are related to needs and values. When you feel satisfied engaging in a particular activity, something about that activity is meeting a need of yours; when you feel dissatisfied, that activity does not fulfill your needs. Activities that consistently make you feel positive (happy, joyful, confident, proud) are therefore more important and valuable to you than activities that leave you feeling negative (upset, sad, mad, disappointed).

Chart 9.1. identifies some of the main needs associated with each of the personal style dimensions. If you score high in a particular dimension, then you most likely will tend to have stronger intensity for the needs listed in that dimension. If you score low in any of the dimensions, most likely you will not have the same intensity for those particular needs as you will for other needs related to your strongest dimensions.

Chart 9.1—Personal Needs According to Personal Style		
	EXTROVERTED	**INTROVERTED**
Task-Oriented	*Behavioral* Achievement Autonomy Power Rewards Stimulation	*Cognitive* Affirmation Order Perfection Respect Understanding
People-Oriented	**AFFECTIVE** Acceptance Attention Expression Recreation Variety	**INTERPERSONAL** Appreciation Harmony Stability Trust Unity

For example, a person who scores high in the behavioral and inter-personal dimensions will have the strong needs associated with those two dimensions. This individual prefers working alone, wants to achieve,and likes material rewards (B), but is also very grateful when others say thanks, are honest, and do not create unpleasant situations (I). If the same person is low in the cognitive and affective dimensions, then most likely he or she will not be as interested in having things organized, getting things done perfectly, or spending time alone with just one person (C); nor will this person have a strong desire to be accepted by others, to spend lots of time at play, or to entertain others (A).

Facing Up to Our Fears

When needs are consistently unfulfilled, fears develop. Needs and fears are opposite sides of the same coin; the reverse of what you need will often constitute what you are afraid of experiencing. For example, since Andy has a strong need for acceptance, he may be prone to a strong fear of rejection. It should be noted that these fears are quite different from those which are triggered by external objects, such as snakes, or from phobias, which are fears deeply rooted in the personality. In every case, these fears have their source in particular needs that over time have gone unmet by people or situations in a person's environment.

Small fears of this type can develop into larger ones if such conditions remain for a long period of time. Individuals who have high levels of fear about something usually have a history of chronic neglect. High-level fears, once established, can have ongoing repercussions in a person's life; they continue to reflect the unmet and intensified needs of the past. Isabella, for example, is probably afraid of speaking in public because her second-grade teacher habitually questioned her honesty in front of her classmates after some milk money was stolen and not recovered. This treatment not only sensitized Isabella's fear of humiliation but also intensified it. Now, years later, she is afraid of any public situation in which there is a chance she will be judged and questioned by a hostile audience.

Needs motivate behavior. In contrast, fears can override or stem our natural impulse to take action. Fears can also provoke less desirable behavior, such as dishonesty and deceit. In short, we move toward and value most whatever meets our needs (pleasure), and we avoid situations where our needs will not be met (displeasure). In addition, if we have a low need for something, not getting it will be less of a threat to us than not getting something that is important. For instance, Bill does not have a high need for approval and therefore has less fear of rejection than Andy, who has a strong need to be accepted.

Chart 9.2 provides a list of the needs and fears of each personal style dimension. As before, you should try to apply this information to yourself according to the areas in which you received the highest scores on the PSI. If you are strong in several dimensions, you will want to integrate the information from each of those areas. For example, Connie scored highest in the cognitive (scoring 55 and 45, respectively) and behavioral dimensions, so she would read the sections for these two dimensions. By examining both lists of needs and fears together, she will have a clearer picture of which ones influence her behavior the most.

Chart 9.2—Typical Personal Fears	
The Behavioral person	*Therefore*
NEEDS:	FEARS:
Achievement	Failure
Autonomy	Restriction
Power	Dependency
Rewards	Poverty
Stimulation	Stagnation
The Cognitive person	*Therefore*
NEEDS:	FEARS:
Affirmation	Disapproval
Understanding	Confusion
Order	Chaos
Perfection	Incompetence
Respect	Humiliation
The Interpersonal person	*Therefore*
NEEDS:	FEARS:
Appreciation	Ungratefulness
Harmony	Conflict
Stability	Instability
Trust	Deception
Unity	Dissention
The Affective person	*Therefore*
NEEDS:	FEARS:
Acceptance	Rejection
Attention	Exclusion
Expression	Repression
Recreation	Boredom and Routine
Variety	Routine

Which Way Do I Go Now?

If you were granted three wishes that were guaranteed to come true, what would you ask for? Would you wish for more money? For an end to world hunger? For a good night's sleep? Perhaps the possible choices are too overwhelming, so let's narrow them down. Suppose you were unfortunate enough to lose almost all your belongings in a house fire while away on vacation. What would you most want to have spared? Think about this for a moment. Try to pare down your choices to only three things.

When we say something has value, we are saying it has importance. The greater the importance for us, the greater the value. In an extreme situation like losing possessions in a house fire, our choice of what we would most like to salvage will reveal much about what we consider most significant in our lives. At such times, our values become very noticeable, and how one person's values can differ from another person's values becomes highlighted.

One person may choose to save something that another would put a long way down on his or her list of priorities. These individuals will have quite different values that correspond to their dissimilar preferences for things. And these preferences are often, although not always, linked to personal style differences. (Preferences, or value differences, can also be linked to a person's family of origin, social and cultural influences or traumatic experiences that have reshaped a person's life.) Of course, certain things are essential for everyone, regardless of any personal style differences, because these things meet our fundamental needs. Simply to stay alive, we all have to obtain enough food, clothing, and shelter. This takes time, and in modern societies it takes a considerable amount of money too. Our ability to satisfy these needs is also affected by our mental and physical health.

The importance we place on meeting these basic needs reveals our primary values. Although the need to gather food for survival is the same for all of us, the value that we place on food in our lives is not; it will vary from one person to another. The value of food to us will increase or decrease depending on how much food we already have. We're very selective about how we share such resources when we have limited amounts of them. There is, for example, only so much time in each day, and we can become very particular about how and with whom we will spend our time if we're under pressure to ration it wisely.

But other factors are involved as well. Even though we are starving, we may be willing to sacrifice some of the few remaining morsels of food to help another person to survive. Our values are linked to more than just meeting our own basic needs; they are also linked to our humanity, our sense of who we are and what personal qualities we feel are important to strive for and to maintain. These concerns can be called our *personal values*. Not only do they have a strong influence on how we choose to behave, but they reveal themselves in the choices that we make.

As there can be considerable variation in our personal values, there can be vast differences between the values we ascribe to the same thing. For example, you may rate "variety" highly. This will be manifested in the number of new experiences and activities that you seek out. It may be revealed in your choosing (or wanting to choose, if you had the money and the opportunity) to travel all over the world, visiting or living in many different countries. In contrast, perhaps I prefer "security." I may desire freedom from debts to other people, from both financial obligations and moral responsibilities. As a result, I may be more likely to avoid risks and to settle for my existing circumstances and routine. This may be reflected in my being content to live in the same house for 20 years.

These differences in values will affect behavior. You may be more willing to take chances than I am, especially ones in which you are risking variety over security. On the other hand, I am more likely to move cautiously when dealing with financial matters, particularly ones that have a long-term impact, such as mortgages and insurance policies. Whether our lives turn out successfully and we achieve happiness and satisfaction is also determined by many other factors, not least of which is the amount of information we have available at the time we make the choices.

A partial list of some typical personal values is shown on page 100, in Chart 9.3. The values are identified in the left-hand column and then defined in the right-hand one. Take a moment to consider which of these personal values are significant for you and in what ways they may affect how you behave and how you make choices in your life.

Chart 9.3—A List of Typical Personal Values

Values	Definitions
Accomplishments —	Completing tasks well; obtaining results.
Acknowledgement—	Being praised for effort and thanked for consideration shown toothers.
Challenge —	Setting targets to achieve; defending opinions; taking part in contests.
Cooperation —	Having people get along well together; family and marital harmony; teamwork.
Creativity —	Being able to experiment with and develop new ideas.
Expertise —	Being knowledgeable about a subject and an expert in a field or skill area.
Friendship —	Making many friends, interacting with them, maintaining contact when apart.
Honesty —	Being, and having others be, truthful.
Independence —	Avoiding restrictions; being free to control one's own destiny.
Instruction —	Learning new information, sharing it with others; teaching.
Intimacy —	Sharing close companionship and deep affection with someone.
Organization —	Having systematic procedures and logical reasons for doing things.
Pleasure —	Being stimulated, feeling excited, and experiencing much laughter and joy.
Quality —	Maintaining a high standard of work with few errors; good service from others.
Recognition —	Striving to become well known, to obtain awards, to achieve a special status.
Responsibility —	Being in charge of self and/or others; organizing events, making decisions.
Security —	Being secure from financial and moral debts.
Tranquility —	Having peace and quiet, a life with few personal conflicts, solitude.
Variety —	Living an active, exciting life which allows for a variety of experiences.
Wealth—	Achieving financial independence and the power of having and spending money.

Most people learn to accept value differences in others as a "fact of life." Yet often when adjustments cannot be made, conflict occurs. Conflict is usually the result of a clash of values that has not been resolved peacefully. Anger often indicates that one or more individuals in a conflict strongly value whatever issue they feel is at stake. People tend to get angry only when something is important to them.

Connie, for example, values expertise. This particular value influences her perfectionism and how it shapes her attitudes toward tasks and people. She wants to be the expert and likes to succeed at whatever she does. She gets quite frustrated when this doesn't happen, because she believes that others will perceive her as a failure. This characteristic often leads Connie into heated discussions when she thinks people are interfering with her methods and plans for doing things. The value she places on expertise influences not only her perceptions and behavior in the work environment but also how well she works with others. She has difficulty working closely with people who do not perform up to her strict work standards, because she doesn't want their shortcomings to reflect badly upon her reputation. Her attempts to control situations often lead to conflict.

Individuals with similar personal style patterns are more likely to have similar values than individuals with contrasting style patterns. It is much easier, therefore, for these sorts of relationship to improve, because there are fewer areas of conflict. But people with contrasting style patterns and different values can develop relationships if they make a conscious effort to understand the other person and to see the environment from the other's point of view.

To develop relationships with people, it is necessary to respect their values, especially when these values are not the same as ours. Marriage counseling often focuses on the differences in values between the two partners. Helping each partner learn how to be more considerate of what is important to the other is often necessary before discussing particular issues of concern.

Isabella, for instance, needs to accept and respect Andy's strong values for pleasure and friendship. If he invites home many more people than she would like to see in the house or spends more money on recreation than she would, she should understand that he is operating in the context of his values. Andy, on the other hand, has to learn to respect Isabella for the value she places on saving money (security) and having time alone with him (tranquility). He must be willing to accept Isabella's values as a reflection of the person she is.

Personal values are very powerful in directing behavior. Most people tend to invest their time and energy in areas that will bring them the most personal rewards. What you consider to be most rewarding is directly related to what is most valuable to you. Consequently, values are like inner goals that each individual hopes to achieve while interacting with others and the environment. An example of this concept in action can be seen when groups of people get together for a collective effort. Teamwork is best accomplished when individuals on the team have common goals and values. Those groups that have members with similar values and goals work better together because motivational drives within the individuals in the group are going in similar directions.

Certain values can be related to particular personal style dimensions, as illustrated by the lists presented in Chart 9.4. These lists represent some of the main values that can be associated with each of the personal style dimensions.

It is safe to say that, given a choice, most of us would probably choose all of the values listed. Yet, because we are limited by the amount of time and energy we have, when we work hard to acquire one value, we often eliminate opportunities to obtain other values. For example, valuing "challenge" might encourage one father, but not another, to seek out personal experiences—such as flying alone to Africa for a vacation—which would take time and resources away from his family. While this meets a personal need of his, it comes at the expense of other family members' needs.

Chart 9.4—Personal Values According to Personal Style

The Behavioral person

NEEDS:	*Therefore* VALUES:
Achievement	Accomplishment
Autonomy	Independence
Power	Responsibility
Rewards	Wealth
Stimulation	Challenge

The Cognitive person

NEEDS:	*Therefore* VALUES:
Affirmation	Intimacy
Understanding	Instruction
Order	Organization
Perfection	Quality
Respect	Expertise

The Interpersonal person

NEEDS:	*Therefore* VALUES:
Appreciation	Acknowledgement
Harmony	Tranquility
Honesty	Security
Stability	Cooperation
Trust	
Unity	

The Affective person

NEEDS:	*Therefore* VALUES:
Acceptance	Friendship
Attention	Recognition
Expression	Creativity
Recreation	Pleasure
Experience	Variety

Let's Play Ball!

It's obvious that playing basketball is a more important activity for individuals who like to play the game than for those who seldom or never choose to play it. People who enjoy this game spend time and energy (values that are constant for all of us) practicing, traveling to and from games, and actually playing. Individuals who do not invest as much of their time and energy in the game may still enjoy it, but not enough to stop participating in other activities that are more important to them. In general, we could say that in regards to basketball, people who seldom play, sometimes play, and often play have differing personal needs when it comes to recreational activities. We might expect those who do play to be linked by the same personal needs; however, this is not necessarily the case. Even when people choose to participate in the same activity, this decision does not always arise from the desire to satisfy the same personal needs. Let's stick with the game of basketball to demonstrate how people with different personal styles tend to be motivated differently even while engaging in the same activity.

Bill Behavioral will play a game as long as there is a *challenge* and he has an opportunity to meet that challenge. He needs to *achieve* his ambitions, and he will frequently compete against himself to satisfy internal goals. Bill tends to be a very consistent performer and plays his hardest every time. Individuals like Bill tend to make good team *leaders* and coaches because they usually understand every facet of the game and like to be in *control*. Bill is quick to forget losses and to focus on upcoming games, as he doesn't like dwelling on the past.

Connie Cognitive plays because she wants to win and to be the best player on the best team. This would meet her strong need for *respect* from others. After a loss, players like Connie can often be very critical of themselves, their coaches and teammates, the umpires, and the members of the other team. Connie also tends to be a *perfectionist* and has *high standards* about how the game should be played. When confident, Connie is *extremely competitive* and plays hard, but when upset due to low-quality playing, either by herself or by her teammates, she tends to sulk and may give up playing.

Isabella Interpersonal plays well because she enjoys being a part of the "family." Players like Isabella usually strive to play their hardest for the team as a whole rather than simply for themselves. This meets their need to give to others and is also a good way for them to be *appreciated* by others. If there is conflict among team members or the coaching staff, Isabella either will try to resolve it quietly or will become depressed and withdrawn because of her strong need for *unity* and *harmony*. She still remains a consistent performer even when feeling upset, as she does not want her feelings to weaken the rest of the team.

Andy Affective is out there for the *pleasure* of playing the game. He likes to have fun; thus he can be a very poor practice player. He will tend to show up late, and tend to horse around when he does arrive. Yet during the game Andy often gives 110 percent. Public *recognition* is very important to Andy, and the glory of winning is a strong motivating force for him. He loves to rise to the occasion when the pressure is on and there is a large audience watching him play. He will also make time to help other players improve their skills and excel to their best because he likes to *influence* others to achieve.

The study of individual differences is fascinating. We discover that what motivates one person doesn't necessarily motivate another. We also see how our inner drive to fulfill our needs can extend beyond our individual pursuits and have a positive or negative effect upon others. One advantage of personal style theory is that can help you understand what motivates you. It identifies your strongest needs, fears, and values. Having such knowledge allows you to develop a deeper sense of self-awareness, but even more importantly, it gives you an awareness and an understanding of how other people are unique.

Knowing more about what motivates you and what motivates others is essential to developing positive relationships. Chapters 11 through 14 will explore how personal style information can help you to achieve more effective relationships with others. But first, let's take a look at how motivation fits into the world of work.

Chapter 10.
Personal Style and the World of Work

The harder I work, the luckier I get.

— Sam Goldwyn

The Internal Factor of Personal Style

Besides the powerful influence personal style has on developing credibility, leadership, and relationships both at home and at work, it has a tremendous effect on each one of us as workers. In the previous chapters I discussed similarities and differences between style dimensions, internal and external compatibility, and motivational differences related to personal style preferences. Now it is time to apply personal style theory to the world of work.

Personal style theory does not provide people with enough information for them to base major career decisions on it, yet this type of information is very useful when evaluating options that are relevant to making such decisions. As people spend a great deal of their lives in work situations, it only makes sense for them to consider those forms of work that best fit their personal styles. For instance, completing work tasks that are suited to your personal style increases the chances that your primary needs will be met. As we read in Chapter 9, when your primary needs are satisfied, you feel happier than when they are unsatisfied. You will also feel motivated to excel in your chosen occupational area, because your needs are being fulfilled.

Occupational planning is well worth your time and effort if it helps you choose a career that will not cost you more than it provides over the long term. Too often individuals accept jobs for reasons related to external factors, such as salary or workplace location, without any consideration of how the job will meet their main needs. Financial security, in particular, can often keep people working in unsatisfying jobs longer than they had originally planned.

For example, young people often have jobs that pay just enough to cover basic living costs, such as rent and making car payments. At first they are content with the freedom and independence their paycheck provides, but after a while, they realize that such jobs do not leave them with enough time to complete the education required by higher-paying jobs; moreover, they find themselves struggling to deal with increasingly high levels of frustration as their inner needs continue to go unmet. This example underscores the necessity for considering both external and internal factors—such as personal style—when doing occupational planning.

The World of Work

The work world includes a variety of jobs, occupations, and careers. Each level of labor calls for certain types of requirements and offers its own particular benefits. These benefits do not necessarily include a salary. Many people volunteer to work for community service organizations, such as food banks, in order to help others; or donate their time to professional organizations, such as hospitals, in order to gain practical experience in a field. Although volunteer work is ordinarily placed in its own category and rarely considered a job, an occupation, or a career in itself, it still calls for the performance of certain tasks and thus should be regarded as a member of the world of work.

The work world is vast and includes all locations where jobs, occupations, and careers are in action. Work environments vary widely, with home-centered occupations on the rise. Advances in computer technology have contributed to this extension of the work environment; for example, word processing is a common home-centered occupation. Service-oriented home-centered businesses, such as day care, are also on the increase as economic and social pressures necessitate the two-paycheck family and single-parent families become more common.

The current trend of extending the work environment into the home is somewhat ironic in that it has led some of us right back to where we first began: to the family setting, the kind of environment where most of us initially learned about work, whether by watching an older brother mow the lawn or Dad paint the fence. As children, many of us came to understand that someone working on a single household job was required to perform a series of tasks. We may have understood these tasks as steps a person would take to do the job correctly. For example, we might have noticed that actually pushing the mower over the lawn was only one step, or one work task, in the job of mowing the lawn, and that the tasks of putting gas in the mower, starting it, and emptying it were also essential to this job. As we grew older, many of us learned to undertake household jobs like this in increments, by helping out and fulfilling certain work tasks, rather than all at once.

In general, *work tasks* form the anatomy of a job; their purpose is to fulfill certain functions that are necessary for the job to be completed successfully. A *job* is an activity that is focused on one purpose: to produce a specific piece of work, such as mowing a lawn, designing an ad, or facilitating a training workshop. Jobs usually involve marketable skills, and all positions of employment actually consist of many jobs that must be performed repeatedly according to their respective time schedules. Some jobs must be carried out daily, for example, whereas others must be completed only bi-weekly or monthly.

An *occupation* is often more complex. It is usually considered a permanent work position that consists of several jobs. Being a gardener, for instance, is an occupation that includes jobs such as mowing the lawn, planting the garden, and pruning the bushes. When occupations are related they usually form a particular field of work.

A *career*, or profession, would be a person's lifework. Careers often consist of one or more occupations. For example, an individual who has a career in landscaping might have started out as a gardener and moved on to training and supervising other gardeners while managing a large land-development company.

The relationship between these elements of the work world can be formulated in the following way:

> **Work Tasks = A Job**
> **Jobs = An Occupation**
> **Occupations = A Career**
> **A Career or Careers = A Lifetime of Work**

Not very long ago most people had careers that primarily focused on one occupational area, such as banking, manufacturing, or education. Individuals in today's world may have a series of completely different careers during a lifetime either by choice or circumstances beyond their control. In fact it is increasingly common for people to complete several different careers before retiring from the work force or to shift from a long-standing career into a new one during midlife. One person I knew spent 20 years in several occupations related to accounting only to change his career and become a successful photographer specializing in weddings and family gatherings. Interestingly enough is estimated that students in high school today will have as many as 15 different occupations before they retire.

Work done with little effort is likely to yield little result.

— B.C. Forbes

Work Tasks

Every job contains a combination of work-related tasks that must be accomplished if the job is to be completed successfully. Most of us prefer to do certain work tasks and not others. This indicates that we have strong personal preferences for how we would like to spend our working hours. For example, you might like working outdoors doing manual labor tasks rather than working indoors sitting at a desk and talking with others. Work-related tasks can be divided into the following four main categories:

1. Things
Many daily tasks involve the use of objects and/or things that were invented to alter the amount of work we must do. A simple example of this is the shovel. With it you can move dirt more easily than if you used your hands, but not more easily than if you use a bulldozer.

Besides working with tools, this category would include preferences for working with machines, animals, plants, raw materials (such as wood or metals), technological equipment, robotics, large corporations, and so forth. Individuals who have a very strong preference for the *behavioral* personal style dimension often prefer careers in this category because they call for high levels of physical energy.

2. Data

This category includes all tasks involved in the use of information. Information comes in many different forms, such as facts, numbers, statistics, and dates. It also encompasses all data-related activities that involve information; for example, programming, recording, filing, planning, or editing. Individuals who have a strong orientation in the *cognitive* personal style dimension are often interested in these kinds of work activities because they involve mental concentration and energy.

3. People

The world of work is made up of many different jobs that require people-related tasks. Jobs that primarily include people-related activities such as teaching, selling, motivating, accommodating, and helping would fit into this category. Work positions in this area focus on assisting people in some area of their daily lives. *Interpersonal-type* individuals are usually so strong in their orientation to people that they are often interested in these types of work tasks.

4. Ideas

The fourth category of work activities deals with ideas and all activities related to thinking and performing creatively. This would include such activities as painting, writing, entertaining, investigative research, and designing. Jobs that primarily focus on ideas require original thinking and the ability to work independently. People who have a strong natural tendency toward the *affective* dimension are usually very creative and intuitive as a result of their high level of creative energy. They like jobs and occupations that allow them to be imaginative in their expression of their ideas and abilities.

Because personal preferences greatly sway your decisions about work, Chart 10.1 on page 110 was created to assist you in seeing some possible relationships between personal style dimensions and work tasks. While the four areas of work activities loosely match up with the four personal style dimensions, they do not match exactly. You have all four dimensions to some degree; and therefore, to some extent, you may enjoy activities that do not fall into the areas of your personal style's stronger preferences.

Chart 10.1—Personal Style Preferences and Work Tasks			
	VERY STRONG	**STRONG**	**MEDIUM**	**LOW**
BEHAVIORAL	Things	Data	Ideas	People
COGNITIVE	Data	Ideas	People	Things
INTERPERSONAL	People	Things	Data	Ideas
AFFECTIVE	Ideas	People	Things	Data

We succeed in enterprises that demand the positive qualities we possess, but we excel in those that can also make use of our defects.

— **Alexis de Tocqueville**

Natural Aptitudes and Limitations

Natural aptitudes are those areas of ability that you instinctively feel most comfortable working with. These areas are usually the same areas in which you acquired most of the skills you have learned in life. Natural limitations include personal areas of weakness or deficits in your particular personal style that can keep you from being successful.

The successful completion of each particular work task requires specific work skills. A *skill* is an acquired behavior that you can consistently perform well in various situations. For example, having the ability to drive large trucks in diverse weather conditions is a skill that is valuable to trucking companies. Understanding your personal style preferences can help you develop natural abilities into skills. The skills that you have learned the most easily during your life probably fit your natural aptitude areas, whereas the ones that have been more difficult for you to learn probably did not.

It is necessary to realize that sometimes your greatest strengths can also become your greatest weaknesses. As you age, you tend to move towards those events and situations in which you are naturally skilled and away from those in which you are less able. In short, you often become very good at what you prefer to do and less productive in what you don't like doing. This can lead you into putting most of your eggs (aptitudes) in fewer baskets (skill areas) until you are stuck with only one or two areas of expertise.

Without other developed skills to fall back on, you could find yourself unemployed if occupations that require your skills cease to exist or if other circumstances force you to change occupational areas. Many types of labor leave workers in midlife with bodies that have given out from long hours of hard work (bad backs, arthritic joints). A prime example of this would be a strong behavioral-type person who, having worked all his life using his hands and body in heavy labor situations, suddenly has to change careers because of a physical injury.

Also, many workers often stop learning about things that are not related to their particular type of work because they assume such knowledge will not be needed. When they are forced to change occupations due to injury or other unforeseeable events, they often lack the confidence necessary to do so. This may occur because they do not have the academic skills (reading, writing, math, studying) or basic occupational knowledge and skills required to retrain for a different career; what they did best in life trapped them into an occupational field in which they had no future.

Skill aptitude strengths and limitations have been listed on the following pages, in Chart 10.2 through Chart 10.5, according to each of the four personal style dimensions. It is important to mention that some of the aptitude areas presented in the charts may be areas that you have never excelled in before, while some of the skill limitations listed may actually be areas of strength for you. These results can occur when physical or social factors in your life have either kept you from developing certain aptitude areas or have forced you to improve in certain skill areas in which you were deficient.

It is no secret that finding a job in today's economic circumstances is not easy. It is just as tough a task whether you have just graduated from high school or are making a career transition after 20 years with the same company. While there are more career choices than ever before, there are also more requirements and job information to consider.

Chart 10.2—Behavioral Aptitudes and Limitations

Aptitudes *Individuals who are strong in the behavioral dimension tend to be naturally good at:*

Learning quickly
Working under pressure
Providing situational help
Working hard
Problem solving
Being time efficient
Planning for the future
Dedication to a cause

Making decisions
Taking risks
Delegating tasks
Dealing with world and environmental
Concerns
Handling responsibility
Working alone
Goal setting

Individuals who score low in this dimension will most likely be naturally weak in the above skill areas.

Areas of Difficulty *Individuals who are strong in this dimension also tend to be:*

Insensitive to other's
 feelings
Stubborn in changing
 their viewpoints
Belligerent when upset
Authoritative
Uncompromising
Unappreciative

Poor teamworkers
Poor subordinate workers
Interpersonal-communication
 avoiders
Socially aggressive
Prideful
Unapologetic
Humorless

Chart 10.3—Cognitive Aptitudes and Limitations

Aptitudes *Individuals who are strong in the cognitive dimension tend to be naturally good at:*

Calculating figures
Organizing data
Attending to details
Proofreading
Maintaining standards
Giving in-depth presentations
Clarifying information
Creating charts and visual aids

Remembering dates
Analyzing details
Researching information
Following instructions
Getting quality results
Being loyal
Creating systems
Applying deductive reasoning

Individuals who score low in this dimension tend be weak in the skills listed above.

Areas of Difficulty *Individuals who are strong in this dimension also tend to:*

Daydream often
Be pessimistic
Be advice-givers
Feel stress when overworked
Ask too many questions
Overreact when angry
Live in the past
Forget people's names

Be too picky
Speak bluntly
Make decisions slowly
Dominate conversations
Be poor listeners
Freeze under pressure
Overworry
Be loners

Chart 10.4—Interpersonal Aptitudes and Limitations

Aptitudes *Individuals who are strong in the interpersonal dimension tend to be good at:*

Working consistently	Greeting the public
Serving others	Taking care of others
Keeping records and filing	Organizing events
Driving	Finishing projects
Ordering supplies	Answering phones
Conserving materials	Being patient
Fixing things	Doing craft work
Constructing things	Listening to others

Individuals who score low in this dimension tend be weak in the above skills.

Areas of Difficulty *Individuals who are strong in this dimension also tend to be:*

Overly sensitive	Shy in front of groups
Generally unassertive	Slow to react
Stubborn when angry	Shortsighted planners
People-pleasers	Overly quiet
Stressed-out by too much responsibility	Tenuous delegators
Too easygoing	Personally unorganized
Verbally noninspirational	Weak disciplinarians
	Indecisive

Chart 10.5—Affective Aptitudes and Limitations

Aptitudes *Individuals who are strong in the affective dimension tend to be:*

Imaginative	Inventive
Energetic	Quick to become involved
Resourceful	Enterprising
Quick to learn when focused	Sensitive to others
Musical	Funny, entertaining
Good group leaders	Persuasive
Inductive reasoners	Artistic
Motivational	

Individuals who score low in this dimension tend to be weak in the above skills.

Areas of Difficulty *Individuals who are strong in this dimension sometimes tend to:*

Start too many projects	
Fail to finish projects	Ignore timelines
Tell lies	Have too many interests
Be unreliable	Be self-centered
Be inconsistent	Manage money poorly
Drive recklessly	Overplay
Become addicted easily	Be unconventional learners
Impulsively make decisions	

There are many obstacles blocking the way to success. One of the biggest obstacles you may encounter is indecision about what type of career is best for you. Becoming clear on what type of career might best satisfy your personal style preferences can assist you in removing this block. It can help you narrow down the choice list to career areas that will reward you for being who you are.

The world of occupations is vast and diverse in its offerings of task- and people-related activities. There are far too many careers to include all of them in this book. What are presented for each of the personal style dimensions are examples of suggested careers that you might consider if you are predominantly strong in one of the personal style dimensions. These examples, which are found in Chart 10.6 through Chart 10.9, have been randomly listed for each style dimension; that is, they are not presented in any particular order of importance.

Obviously, if you have style flexibility, more than one job in several of the dimension areas will be of interest to you. If you become aware of an occupation that interests you and it is not listed in one of your strongest personal style dimensions, do not discard it. It is important for you to investigate that career area before you make a decision about it.

You should consider the information in all of the dimensions, regardless of how you scored on the PSI, rather than just select one dimension to focus on. Also, you should not pursue a career based solely on the following information. While personal style is one vital criterion to use in such a career search, other factors such as educational requirements, future outlook, financial rewards, and personal abilities should also be considered. Taking a series of career tests or a career exploration course is a good way to locate jobs that best fit your personal preferences. Interviewing others who are employed in jobs that interest you can also be a practical way to obtain such information.

There is something that is much more scarce, something rarer than ability. It is the ability to recognize ability.

— **Robert Half**

Chart 10.6—Occupational Suggestions for Behaviorals

Order of Preference for Work Tasks:
1. Things   2. Data   3. Ideas   4. People

Carpenter	Forest ranger	Police officer
Civil engineer	Draftsperson	Heavy-equipment
Industrial arts	Airline pilot	operator
Fire fighter	Jeweler	Aircraft mechanic
Mechanic	Electrician	Farmer
Mining engineer	Ship pilot	Veterinarian
Surveyor	Dentist	Construction worker
Physician	Game warden	Auto engineer
Surgeon	Locksmith	Tool and die maker
Typesetter	Bank manager	Meat-packer
Lawyer	Administrator	Appliance repairperson
Plumber	Logger	Computer
Welder	Publisher	Ambulance driver
Chemist	General	Company president
Repairperson	Judge	Movie projectionist
		Computer scientist

Chart 10.7—Occupational Suggestions for Cognitives

Order of Preference for Work Tasks:
1. Data   2. Ideas   3. People   4. Things

Accountant	Data typist	Dental assistant
Statistician	Proofreader	Estimator
Cashier	Court reporter	Credit manager
Loan officer	Bookkeeper	Clerk
Travel agent	Librarian	Legal secretary
Mail carrier	Postal worker	Funeral director
Cargo agent	Motel manager	Controller
Executive secretary	Butler	Medical-records worker
Appraiser	Auditor	Insurance underwriter
Research analyst	Historian	Library assistant
Academic advisor	Mathematician	Movie/art critic
Credit analyst	Economist	Quality control technician
Pharmacist	Geographer	Prosecutor
Claims adjuster	Meteorologist	Food/drug inspector
Tax assessor	Bibliographer	Dental technician

Chart 10.8—Occupational Suggestions for Interpersonals

Order of Preference for Work Tasks:
   1. People   2. Things   3. Data   4. Ideas

Registered nurse	Social worker	Day-care supervisor
Secretary	Beautician	Social scientist
Music teacher	Interpreter	Receptionist
Dental hygienist	Host/hostess	Mental-health worker
Waiter/waitress	Word processor	Telephone operator
Bank teller	Counselor	Child-welfare worker
Driving teacher	Homemaker	Recreation therapist
Social director	Chiropractor	Speech pathologist
Flight attendant	Minister	General typist
Dietitian	Stenographer	Parking attendant
Audiologist	Custodian	Medical lab technician
Bus driver	Tailor	Health inspector
Optometrist	Biologist	Bacteriologist
Psychologist	Missionary	Elementary teacher
Physiotherapist	Special ed. teacher	
Truck driver		

Chart 10.9—Occupational Suggestions for Affectives

Order of Preference for Work Tasks:
   1. Ideas   2. People   3. Things   4. Data

Auctioneer	Entertainer	Pastor
Artist	Model	Interior decorator
Photographer	Broadcaster	Physical education teacher
Fashion designer	Disk jockey	Secondary teacher
Cartoonist	Architect	Personnel officer
Sign painter	Bartender	Public-relations worker
Actor/actress	Dancer	Newspaper reporter
Singer	Announcer	Hair stylist
Author	Florist	Marketing executive
Landscaper	Buyer	Restaurant manager
Stockbroker	Promoter	Music arranger
Musician	Philosopher	Foreign-relations worker
Drama teacher	Politician	Journalist
Business agent	Composer	
Physicist	Real estate agent	
Salesperson	Gourmet chef	

Skills for Future Success

Besides the skills related to personal style development, there are some specific skills you need to develop if you want to be in high demand in the future. Future predictions indicate that there will be many major shifts within the world of work in the next decade. The beginning of such shifts are rapidly appearing in the economies of the world.

For example, the center of the financial world is now located in Tokyo rather than in Europe or America. It is also noteworthy that more North American trade crosses the Pacific Ocean than the Atlantic. In addition, many of yesterday's major manufacturing services are now located in underdeveloped countries where labor is less expensive. These and other trends have many futurists claiming most employment in the future will fall into the following five career areas:

1. Services
2. Information
3. Tourism
4. Entertainment/Recreation
5. Space–and ocean–related technology

Those individuals who want to be employed in a high salary position will need to have the knowledge and skills required for the job. Those individuals without the necessary education will run a greater risk of working for less money or being unemployed. A higher education is now positively correlated with higher earnings. It is essential that effective skills be developed if career-seekers want to be competitive in their career search.

Regardless of what your personal style pattern is, you will need skills to succeed in the world of work. The following is a quick list of 15 skill areas that are presently highly valued within the work world.

1. Self-Management Skills

Self-management involves all skills that are related to self-control. Having these skills increases your effectiveness when interacting with others. Examples of this type of skill would be telling the truth, controlling your temper, being polite, dressing appropriately, and having patience. While these skills will not get you work, not having them can keep you from being hired.

2. Coping Skills

These skills are behaviors that help you deal with pressure and stress. Situations in life often leave individuals feeling overwhelmed. Successfully managing stressful life situations requires skills such as developing support relationships, knowing where to get help if needed, not overreacting to problem situations, and being resourceful. Coping skills help you keep the pressure at "arm's length" so that you have a chance to problem-solve and make decisions.

3. Assertiveness Skills

Assertiveness is often equated with aggressiveness, which is far from the truth. Aggressiveness occurs when you get what you need or want at the expense of others. Assertiveness is the ability to get what you need or want without disrespecting or hurting others. Skills in this area would include speaking appropriately when telling others how you are feeling and what is important to you, saying no to people who are pressuring you into doing something, and asking for what you need.

4. Problem-Solving Skills

Knowing how to solve daily problems takes skill. People who can work through difficult dilemmas and situations tend to be more successful and happy in life than those who can't. A major factor in problem-solving is long-range planning. Many problems arise from short-sighted planning and could be avoided with more follow-through. Skills like editing, estimating, analyzing, calculating, and investigating can help you solve problems and lower the chances of creating situations in the future that will lead to additional problems.

5. Decision-Making Skills

One thing which is certain about the present age we live in, and which will probably hold true in the future, is that life is more complex than ever before. Technology has exacerbated the pressures in daily living. If you have trouble making decisions now, you may experience more stress as time goes on because you will be required to make more decisions in less time. These daily decisions must be made if you are to interact effectively within society. Decision-making skills such as accurately assessing situations, weighing information, evaluating alternatives, considering short-and long-range costs and gains, and making a commitment are some examples of decision-making skills.

6. Communication Skills — Written and Oral

Over the last generation, written and oral skills have become increasingly important, yet it is increasingly difficult to find employees with these skills. Skills such as reading, spelling, writing, word usage, editing, and public speaking are valuable in many work settings. With the information age coming to power within the marketplace, the ability to communicate effectively will become a more valuable skill and a more common requirement for employment.

7. Interpersonal Communication Skills

With jobs getting harder to obtain, the ability to impress others will be of greater importance. Having good interpersonal communication skills is one way of showing others that you are ready and willing to be a productive part of their work team. Such skills also help you develop relationships with customers, co-workers and supervisors. Such skills can be of even bigger benefit in other areas of life such as marriage, parenting, and doing public or community service. Centering, attending, checking for accuracy, active listening, confrontation, and responding with understanding are a few skills of this type.

8. Job Search Skills

Finding work and convincing others that you are the best person for the job has never been easy, but in the future it will become even more difficult. Having the skills necessary for obtaining work can be a real plus for you, as many people lack skills of this type. Writing resumes and covering letters, identifying job prospects, initiating contact with potential employers, and successful interviewing would be examples of job search skills.

9. Job Maintenance Skills

Obtaining work is one thing; not getting fired is another. With more and more people wanting to work, employers do not have to settle for less than the best, and as the number of workers increases in the future, they will become even more demanding and evaluative. Skills such as time management, consistent work performance, being trustworthy, being trainable and other skills like these will often determine which employee stays and which one goes.

10. Computer Skills

Most jobs in the future will have something to do with computers. Having a basic working knowledge and skill level will even be mandatory for many low-skilled jobs. Programming, word processing, analyzing data, taking inventory, and many other computer-related skills will be needed in the work force, and individuals with skills of this type will be given preference in hiring.

11. Research Skills

Since information and knowledge will be of primary value in the future, all jobs that involve inquiries of any kind will require research skills. These skills will help you learn how to locate up-to-date information and how to utilize it in a manner that will be valuable to others. Research skills include investigating, studying, compiling, organizing, and presenting information; conducting statistical analysis; and knowing how to use a library.

12. Leadership Skills

It can sometimes be difficult to find individuals who have the requirements necessary to be effective leaders. It takes both personal characteristics and knowledge to guide others successfully. Leaders must have many of the skill areas that have been previously mentioned, such as decision-making skills and communication skills. In addition, they also need to demonstrate administrative skills, the ability to delegate, group process skills, and organizational skills.

A complete list of 56 of the most important skills required to lead effectively can be found in Anderson's *Transforming Leadership* (1992). This book, along with the *Leadership Skills Inventory*, can provide you with a detailed look at skill development that will enhance your present leadership abilities regardless of personal style (see note on page 53 for more information).

13. Instructional/Training/Facilitation Skills

The ability to teach others what you know will be a very marketable skill in the future. To do this with success, skills such as lesson planning, presenting information, using educational aids, testing, modeling, giving feedback, and evaluating will be needed. While many workers are proficient in their jobs, they don't always have the skills to help train new employees. Having group process skills will make you a valuable asset to any employer.

14. Cross-Cultural Skills

As previously mentioned, more and more business is being conducted in international markets. Individuals with knowledge and skills related to different cultures will be sought after. Having skills such as speaking and writing in different languages, understanding different customs and religions, and establishing a network of contacts in foreign countries can be to your advantage in finding work.

15. Entrepreneurial Skills

While not everyone is capable of going out and starting their own business, this type of employment is currently on the increase. Many jobs in the future will be service-oriented. Success in your own business will require most of the skills previously mentioned and others such as selling yourself and your ideas, acquiring working capital, accurate market analysis, production and promotion of services, and accounting and financial planning.

Entrepreneurial Characteristics

As entrepreneurialship is becoming a stronger force in the work world, it is appropriate to discuss briefly the characteristics that fit the successful entrepreneur. Although it is commonly believed that this type of individual starts out independently wealthy, with few obstacles standing in the way of success, this is not true in most cases. Many entrepreneurs have had to work very hard for long periods of time to succeed.

According to *Fortune* magazine, many of the 500 wealthiest individuals in the United States are self-made millionaires who started out with little more than an idea. It is possible to develop your thoughts and build fortunes on them if you have the drive and vision necessary to succeed. Such vision includes the particular certainty that there is, or will be, a demand for your products.

Successful entrepreneurs are equipped with drive and mission. They are often independent, visionary, money-wise, resourceful, quick to make decisions, adept (and thus influencial) with people, well organized, and willing to make the personal sacrifices necessary to succeed. They have a strong work orientation and a clear understanding of what it is they want to accomplish.

Individuals who have strong extroverted tendencies, such as Bill and Andy, have more natural ability to think and act in an entrepreneurial manner. Individuals who have strong behavioral and affective dimensions in their personal style patterns are not afraid of the risks it takes to be successful. The behavioral dimension helps individuals to be task-oriented, to work long hours, to make quick decisions and to do future planning—all qualities that are essential to a successful entrepreneur. The affective dimension, on the other hand, gives the individual other valuable qualities, such as creativity for vision and planning, verbal skills for promoting, and a strong people orientation for networking and marketing. An individual who is strong in both of these dimensions has a good beginning for developing an entrepreneurial career. (Please note, that though just being strong in these two dimensions is not enough: skills, resources, and opportunities are also necessary ingredients of success.)

If you are not strong in either the behavioral or the affective dimension, it will be more difficult, but not impossible, for you to think and act in an entrepreneurial fashion. You can learn to develop the skills required to succeed as an entrepreneur, however, if you are willing to work hard. There are many seminars in the business world today that can provide such assistance.

If you do not feel comfortable with such tasks, it is possible to hire individuals who have strong behavioral and affective abilities. These individuals can take your ideas and develop them into successful business ventures if you are willing to allow them the freedom to do so. (For an in-depth analysis of the characteristics of successful entrepreneurs and to measure your natural tendencies, look into the *Entrepreneurial Style and Success Indicator*. See note, page 53.)

PART FOUR

SKILLS
FOR DEVELOPING
CREDIBILITY

Chapter 11.
Principles for Success

It is never possible to understand completely any other human being; and no individual will ever really understand himself—the complexity is too great.

— **Edward Hall**

Unlocking Your Style

You may be wondering, Well, if my personal style is an inherent part of who I am, how can I do anything about it? What's the point of knowing about something I can't change? If style seems to be so complex, what can I do about it?

It's easy to feel trapped by your style and to believe that all you can do is accept who you are and that attempts to change anything about your attitudes or behavior will be futile. But, in fact, letting yourself fall into this way of thinking is the real trap. The only way you will feel imprisoned by your personal style is if you let yourself be controlled by it. The walls of this prison will be of your own making.

Personal style tendencies are like habits. We naturally behave in these ways without appreciating what we are doing and without realizing that we have alternatives. Once we open ourselves up to the possibility that we actually do have choices, we allow ourselves the opportunity to notice just how many habits are influencing our present behavior. If you always choose the same items from a restaurant menu or always pick the same flavor of ice cream, then you are limiting not just your experience but also the range of possible experiences that can happen to you.

Personal styles can be developed. They need not remain static. We can control their influence and harness their power to bring about significant changes in ourselves and the quality of our relationships with others. But where is the key that unlocks the door to personal style development? Is it within our grasp?

The key *is* within our grasp — in ourselves— and the power to grasp it lies in our willingness to see life from another point of view, our willingness to open ourselves up to the possibility that we can change our timeworn habits, and our willingness to believe that some changes for the better can be made. And if we want to develop more effective relationships with others, we must overcoming our self-centeredness and learn how to accept the differences between other people and ourselves.

None of this is easy, and results do not occur overnight—they happen gradually. To gain some understanding of how success can be achieved, let's explore six basic principles that can help us build a solid foundation for success.

1. Accept others as you accept as yourself.
2. Attempt to bring others closer to you.
3. Focus on the behavior, not the person.
4. Recognize that others have free will.
5. Understand how others view things.
6. Concentrate on giving, not receiving.

Like all good lists, this one is selective. There is much wisdom in our world, and I do not claim to have a monopoly on it; however, based on many years of counseling experience, lengthy discussions with other professionals, and an ever-growing reservoir of observations of human nature in action, I feel that these principles point the best way forward. They offer the most realistic framework within which to discuss the development of personal style. They also provide some necessary guidelines for how to utilize information about personal style in a productive manner. They are worth exploring in detail.

1. Accept others as you accept yourself.

It is easy to pick holes in other people's personalities, wishing they wouldn't say certain things or wouldn't have annoying little habits and idiosyncrasies. Worse still, we tend to judge other people according to how well they reflect our own image. We blame them for not behaving as we would behave under the same circumstances. We want them to live up to our ideals, and we can be too quick to criticize when they fall short of our expectations. If they complain, we call them selfish and uncooperative.

Many arguments in the home or unpleasant experiences at work are generated by our annoyance at other people for not living up to our expectations or seeing things our way. We may feel self-assured that we are actually helping them by telling them off or reproving their faults, but we are only kidding ourselves; all we are really doing is trying to bolster our own view of the universe and how things should operate.

It would be far more beneficial for us to try to understand why people are behaving as they are—to stop and consider that they may have information that we lack or may simply hold different, and justifiable, views of the facts. Invariably, though, the reason why we have difficulty getting along with certain individuals or find particular aspects of a friend or family member's behavior bothersome is that these people have values, needs, and fears that differ from ours. They perceive, approach, and interact with the environment around them in ways that we're not naturally predisposed to understanding. In other words, they possess different personal styles.

Just as you should accept your own personal style, so should you accept the personal style of other people. When you find yourself focusing on an aspect of another person's behavior that you find irritating, try to assess what you think his or her underlying personal style might be; if you can determine what a person's style is, then it becomes possible for you to appreciate what is motivating the person to behave that way. Acceptance is easier when it's preceded by understanding—it is very hard to accept things that we do not yet comprehend.

This does not mean you have to accept everything about another person or that you have to tolerate all of their actions toward you. You have a right to be treated with respect too, and you have a responsibility not to let others abuse you or trample all over your feelings. People have to follow existing codes of behavior and should live up to the moral expectations that people living in the same society have generally agreed upon. They must play the game by the rules. But we must be aware that they may value elements of the game that we consider unimportant, and may interpret some of the rules differently than we do. They may even prefer to play another game. We have to accept that.

With acceptance not only is our own stress level reduced, but the pressure we are exerting on others subsides. When other people recognize we accept them—especially when we accept their different values, needs, and fears—they interpret this as a sign of respect. As we all know, mutual respect helps to bind relationships together and make them strong, while disrespect tends to erode relationships.

2. Attempt to bring others closer to you.

In the "me" society we presently live in, we often tend to care about others for what they can do for us rather than for who they really are. We focus on the "payoff" that we personally get from our relationship with them. We seek to have our needs satisfied, our values met, and our fears calmed. Ironically, we are more likely to achieve this sort of self-gratification if we also address other people's values, needs, and fears at the same time. Sustaining good relations with others involves recognizing the "payoff" that other people are looking for and helping them achieve it. We must aim for a win-win scenario. This basic truth has echoed through the pages of self-help books for years.

However, learning how to care for others in a way that meets their needs is far from easy. It often involves the other person's deliberate cooperation because a realistic compromise must be reached. Sometimes this almost seems impossible; the differences of opinion or the different outlooks can be diametrically opposed and mutually exclusive. In situations like this, where one person can win only at the expense of the other person losing, both have to set their sights lower and look for an amicable resolution. The only way out of this difficulty is to establish a deliberate compromise that takes both parties' needs and values into account. How does this work in practice?

Take, for example, Arthur and his wife, Carmen. Arthur, who like Andy has a strong affective dimension, enjoys chatting and socializing with others because he is people-oriented and needs attention and acceptance. This dimension also influences his attitude toward money, which he is apt to spend freely with little regard for the financial needs of the future. Both these areas of behavior have led to conflict between him and Carmen, who like Connie has a strong cognitive dimension and prefers privacy and financial planning. Neither spouse can quite comprehend the other's preferences, which often results in mutual pain and anger. For instance, just as Arthur may feel hurt and irritated by Carmen's refusal to join him at social events, she may feel hurt and irritated by his leaving her alone to go to them. Whenever Arthur agrees Carmen should stay at home, bitterness and resentment result because she doesn't want him to leave her; she wants him to stay with her at home. The misunderstanding leaves both individuals without their needs being met which creates conditions for further problems to develop in the relationship.

As in our example of Andy and Isabella's marriage (in Chapter 9), the first step in a situation like this is mutual acceptance. Each spouse must realize that the other is not intentionally trying to cause problems but simply acting according to who he or she is; moreover, both must realize that despite their lack of intention, they are hurting each other and making each other feel unloved. Mutual acceptance will be far easier if Arthur and Carmen try to understand the needs underlying each other's actions and then recognize those needs by showing signs of caring (placing the needs of the other over one's own). Carmen, for example, might spend more time in conversation with Arthur or accompany him to social events that are particularly important to him. He, in turn, could cut down on his phone conversations and stay at home on nights when his presence is especially important to her.

This kind of compromise—"give-and-take"—can also be established in the financial area of their marriage. Because Carmen has a strong cognitive dimension, she often independently makes decisions and plans for the future, as she needs freedom and achievement. Arthur must recognize that she has a need to take financial risks, and although he would not take them, he must trust her expertise.

In turn, she could show respect and support for Arthur by letting him have more input into financial decisions. She also could realize that his need to spend money freely does not mean he doesn't care about her or disapproves of what she is planning and saving for. Letting him in on the financial plans for the future can help him to understand better why current spending has to be limited.

3. Focus on the behavior, not the person.

If personal style is as fixed within the personality as it appears to be, then, as we have seen, it is very important that you do not attempt to change others and pressure them to think and to behave according to your preferences. This will only frustrate them and lower your level of credibility with them. It is far more effective to concentrate on understanding how and why they are different and to shift your style to fit their style whenever possible. In doing so, they will feel more understood and cared about, and, in turn, they will be more willing to "shift" their behavior toward your style.

This means we should concentrate on influencing our own behavior by first recognizing what it is about other people's behavior that we don't understand and find annoying. We need to know what irks us. We need to be able to point to it and say, "That's what is bothering me!" Rather than attacking the whole person and criticizing him or her personally, we need to focus on precisely what behavior is at issue for us.

Child psychologists continually stress that one of the golden rules of good parenting is to chastise the child's behavior, not the child. It is much better to say, "Johnny, you again forgot to take off your dirty shoes when you came in from the yard. Will you please try harder to remember next time? You can see they make bad marks on the carpet that have to be cleaned up" than to say, "Johnny, you make me so angry! You messed up the carpet again. Why do you have to annoy me? You never remember to take off your dirty shoes when you come in." The second approach, which by focusing on Johnny interprets the act as a sign of personal inadequacy, leaves the child feeling like a failure and unloved. With this kind of communication, the chances are far greater that the child will personalize the parent's anger and feel angry at the parent than learn the lesson about not coming in with dirty shoes. The first response implies unacceptance of the dirty shoes, not rejection of the child. This leaves the child more open to the suggestion and more willing to comply with the request.

After we have isolated the particular behavior that is bothering us, we must focus on controlling our own natural reactions to that behavior before attempting to resolve it. Our own needs often make this quite difficult; at times they can sabotage our efforts to stay focused on the behavior rather than on the person, and they can forcefully reassert themselves, intensifying our desire to control the situation rather than ourselves. Nonetheless, by making the effort to take charge of our needs and reactions, we send a powerful signal that we desire the other person to behave differently. By deliberately acting "out of character" in a given circumstance, we demonstrate that we are willing to change, and in doing so, often behave in ways that become attractive to that person and further encourage behavior modification and compromise. In telling ourselves what to do rather than telling the other person what to do, we also experience firsthand just how difficult a task we're asking of that person, which in itself can improve the relationship.

Take the example of Connie's husband, Isaac, who like Isabella is strong in the interpersonal dimension. He seldom overrules his wife's plans because he has a high need for harmony in the relationship. He lets her make all the decisions—rather than "rock the boat" by expressing his own opinions—even if he strongly disagrees with her. By doing this, Isaac enables Connie, with her strong cognitive style, to take charge quickly and thus meet her own need to be in control. Initially the resulting harmony is well worth the price to Isaac; however, over time the situation changes. Connie loses respect for her husband because he seems weak and indecisive to her. She becomes even more controlling, and Isaac finds it increasingly difficult to maintain the harmony he needs.

The negative consequences of Isaac's approach to keeping peace in the family lead him deeper and deeper into a life of quiet desperation. Any comment on Connie's behavior results in his backing down from his position or in an argument loaded with verbal attacks launched on both sides, from which he must flee, to his study or the city park—anywhere he can find peace and quiet. In constantly grasping for harmony and misdirecting his efforts, he has no hope of bringing about any changes in this relationship. Yet, by suspending his need for harmony and truly stepping forward to assert himself, holding his ground even if Connie doesn't like it, he can actually initiate a rebuilding of their relationship, however difficult it is for him to "act out of character." In time, if his opinions are sound, she will perceive him as strong and will respect him, thus becoming more willing to recognize his needs and deepen their relationship. The harmony he so desires will not have to be clutched at; it will become a natural consequence of the quality of his relationship with Connie.

Worth pointing out here is that simply because two people are married, it does not necessarily mean they are continuing to develop their relationship. Too often, after years of marriage, individuals grow apart and lose respect for what makes their spouse unique and special. When this occurs, they often forget how to work best together for the good of the relationship. Coexistence can be detrimental to the relationship if one or both of the partners stop trying, because this change often leads to bitterness and resentment. The longer a problem continues, the more difficult it will be to reach a resolution, and eventually the problem will become permanent.

Besides taking appropriate aim, good timing is also significant. Also, there is little point in trying to adapt your behavior when the other person is likely to be unresponsive. For instance, if that person is abusive, aggressively hitting, or threatening you, then you have to take action against the aggressive behavior by getting outside help as soon as possible. Allowing inappropriate, and possibly illegal, behavior to continue in the relationship is the sure way to lead a life of misery.

Putting such extremes aside, it is important to learn how to love the other person while still rejecting his or her inappropriate behavior. This is difficult to do, but not impossible. When someone is behaving in a negative way around you, try to stop all reactions to the inappropriate behavior and ask yourself, "What does this person need right now?" By doing this you may realize how to care for people in a way that is meaningful to them. When people have their needs met, they are often more willing to listen to your concerns about their behavior.

4. Recognize that others have free will.

Instead of blaming other people for their own faults, we sometimes blame ourselves. We claim that things could have, should have, or would have been different if only we had behaved some other way. Sometimes there may be more than a grain of truth in this feeling. But we need to avoid feeling guilty for other people's mistakes and taking responsibility for other people's shortcomings.

Parents are particularly prone to the "if only" syndrome, perhaps because they are so directly involved in the shaping of their children's lives. Parents are the first and the most influential teachers children have as they grow up. Fortunately, most of them are aware of their significance. Indeed, helping children to develop physically, emotionally, mentally, and spiritually is one of the greatest responsibilities any person can ever have. It is also a golden opportunity to improve upon what was done for you when you were a child.

But each life brought into the world develops into a separate individual with his or her own will. Philosophers may argue about whether people really have free will or whether everything is determined by our genetic inheritance, upbringing, and past experiences, yet we don't need to become bogged down in this controversy. Even if our will is not truly free, it is free enough to exert its influence. We can and do make decisions, and society rightly holds us accountable for them. Johnny can choose to drink his cup of milk, or he can choose to throw it on the floor. The older he becomes, the more significant his choice is. Just as he needs to learn to take responsibility for controlling his actions, we need to avoid shouldering the responsibility for him.

In spite of best parental efforts, children will do what they want to and will suffer the consequences. Sensible parenting does not guarantee that a child will be good. Parents sometimes accept too much responsibility for the failures of their children, blaming themselves for what their children freely choose to do. They could do their children and themselves a big favor by placing the responsibility for a child's actions where it belongs—with the child. This approach helps children learn how to take personal responsibility for their behavior instead of avoiding responsibility and blaming others for their own poor choices.

Having said this, let me repeat that individual perceptions, preferences, and behaviors differ between people and are due to many social and environmental factors. One of these differences is personal style. Children have preferred styles of dealing with the environment, and this will affect their behavior.

As youngsters, extroverts like Andy and Bill are going to be more prone to doing what they want to do without first asking their parents for permission. Introverted children, such as Isabella and Connie, will be more likely to ask for permission before doing something. (Remember, either gender can be extroverts or introverts.) It is also likely that extroverted children will be more strong-willed than introverted children and, therefore, may require firmer guidelines and reinforcements.

Since children have less well developed self-concepts than adults, lack emotional stamina, and need encouragement to reflect on the relation between causes and effects, they often need our help at appreciating how preferences due to personal style differences may be influencing their behavior. We can assist them to understand this phenomenon, but we will not help them at all if we deny their own will and use the concept of personal style as a crutch to support their improper behavior. Having a preferred style of dealing with life is not a sufficient excuse for anything.

5. Understand how others view things.

You have probably heard the adage, "Don't criticize the way someone walks until you have journeyed ten miles in his moccasins." I don't know whether any Native American ever actually said this, but the image of someone hobbling down the road in ill-fitting shoes tends to encapsulate the problem beautifully. We all have a habit of judging other people according to our own standards and of assuming that everyone should see the world from our point of view. One of the most significant advantages of learning about personal style is that we come to appreciate how differently other people see the world. This knowledge gives us the opportunity to wear other people's moccasins.

We desperately need to try on these moccasins if we are to understand why people walk along such different paths. Again, this is especially true for parents. They often attempt to mold children to fit their view of life. This can have a positive effect when the focus stays on teaching children skills, values, and morals for living. It is the responsibility of the parent to educate the child in these areas and to prepare him or her for making the larger decisions in life. Yet, too often parents offer this instruction strictly from their own point of view, failing to stop and think about how the child perceives the situation and the environment.

Be aware there are different ways to teach your children what you want them to learn. The real challenge of parenting is in matching your style of teaching to your child's style of learning. Children often understand that what parents are telling them is important, and even sometimes go so far as to agree with them. But this verbal agreement does not necessarily guarantee that children are going to behave as their parents want them to when actually placed in situations of choice.

For example, Isabella might teach her high-behavioral child Bianca to be "seen and not heard," which fits the child's personal style, as she is not verbally oriented to begin with. Yet, Isabella might also complain that Bianca does what she thinks is best and seldom asks for her mother's approval. Even though Bianca gives the impression of being compliant, she is really a very independent decision-maker who knows what she wants out of life and does not stand around waiting for permission to go and get it; therefore, Isabella needs to set some guidelines for her to follow and must explain the consequences of breaking these guidelines. When she does break the rules, the consequences must be applied every time or Bianca will not perceive Isabella as being in control. When parents are not in control, extroverted children such as Bianca take control quickly.

6. Concentrate on giving, not receiving.

Most of us are attracted to other people because they have characteristics that we admire, such as being funny or highly skilled at some type of task. Often we decide to marry individuals who can do things we cannot do well. This tendency is reflected in the saying, "Opposites attract." But after getting married, we soon find out who the person really is beneath the surface, and sometimes we experience an emotional letdown or a sense of disappointment because the individual's perceived area of strength is now experienced as an area of concern.

Marriage counselors frequently observe that the traits a husband and wife list on paper as the reasons why they were first attracted to each other in the first place are the same ones they later state as sources of disagreement. For example, when Alice was asked why she decided to marry Bill, she commented, "Well, he had a strong personality, was good with money, and made quick decisions." When Bill in turn was asked why he was initially attracted to Alice, he replied, "Well, she was easy to talk with, caring toward others, and let me make up my own mind."

During counseling, however, Alice revealed precisely how these strengths had become annoying limitations for her. She described how angry she had become with Bill because he was too dominant ("a strong personality"), seldom let her spend money ("good with money") and usually didn't let her know what decisions he was making regarding their business affairs ("makes quick decisions"). Bill, on the other hand, was upset with Alice because she was frequently either visiting friends or talking on the phone ("easy to talk with"), was overly sensitive about other people's feelings ("caring toward others") and didn't respond much when he told her what he was going to do ("lets me make up my own mind").

This relationship could be looked at from several different points of view. How did their own families tend to resolve problems? Are there other "hidden" issues that make these two behave toward each other the way they do? Do they need the assistance of a financial consultant to help them learn how to manage their money problems more effectively? Approaches of this type are important, but they will most likely not help the two individuals learn how to accept, respect, and love each other more effectively.

The key to marriage and parenting is learning how to support each other in love, especially at times when you do not want to. This involves encouraging the other person verbally and nonverbally with messages and behaviors that are comforting and based on his or her personal style rather than your own. Love is giving of oneself to another; it is not self-centered, but other-centered. Love does not blackmail or hold others for ransom, which means if your partner or child is not doing what you want them to do, you do not withhold your love from them.

In practice, this involves viewing the relationship and each area of concern in it from a personal style perspective. Let's return to the situation that faced Bill and Alice. As their counselor, I might assess Alice as being strong in the affective and interpersonal dimensions because she likes to talk with others frequently (A), is sensitive toward people (A and I), and becomes quiet when discussing important issues (I). Bill sounds like he is predominantly strong in the behavioral dimension. I would guess this because he makes quick decisions (B), is future-oriented in his planning (B), and works independently from his wife in all of his financial decision-making (B).

During counseling I would help Alice understand why Bill tends to behave as he does, why he prefers to take the actions he takes, and what it is about people with behavioral styles that makes them act the way they do. In doing this I would explain needs, values, and fears. I would assist Bill in a similar way, trying to help him realize why Alice behaves as she does. The difficult part would then be to help each person stop trying to change the other person's personal style pattern. I would try to help them find areas of agreement and help them build upon these areas by developing strategies for behaving together in set situations.

An example would be assisting them in keeping their checkbook balanced. Alice tends to forget to record many of the checks she writes because she is often talking with people around her at the time of the purchase. She is people-oriented and needs attention and acceptance: talking is a better way to get these needs met than writing is. Bill, on the other hand, never misses an entry in the checkbook because he is task-oriented and always figures out their monthly statements. In this situation, I would suggest that Alice put a large picture of Bill inside the checkbook so that when she is talking she will see him and remember he needs to have the correct information. In turn, I would ask Bill to let Alice figure out the checkbook every third month or so, to let her realize how difficult it is when the checkbook is incomplete.

By helping these two individuals understand and appreciate each other's styles and strengths, a bond of respect can be built from their differences, replacing the wedge those differences formed as sources of stress in the relationship. Developing a willingness to learn from each other and an acceptance of each other "as is" creates a climate within which a more constructive approach toward solving problems can thrive.

Our next step is twofold: to explore in more detail how this process can improve relationships and to consider the problem of how we can develop credibility in a relationship. How does knowledge of personal style theory help us here? The next chapter will discuss this topic; however, before we move on, we must touch upon one last important detail: progress.

A Word About Progress

It's been said many times that there is no gain without pain. It has also been said many times that the difference between winning and losing is not giving up. Perhaps that is stretching things a little too far, but it is no exaggeration to say that trying to live up to a set of principles is not easy. Learning to behave differently can be frustrating at times, even very stressful. It's difficult to exercise self-control over your attitudes and behaviors, especially deep-seated natural preferences.

It's a process that takes time and practice. It can't be hurried. Yet, if it's worth having, it's worth striving for and it's worth waiting for. The important thing is to try to make some recognizable progress and to then to acknowledge that your efforts have succeeded, even if only partially. This will reinforce the value of putting forth the effort in the first place and make you more willing to try again. Everything hangs on having the courage to try.

Chapter 12.
Build Credibility Through Effectiveness

Nothing wins friends so much as an unselfish concern on our part. Nothing makes us so worthy of friendship as developing ourselves, our resources, our personality by a program of friendliness and usefulness to others.

— James A. Magner

Trust is the Name of the Game

You have probably been in a situation where a salesperson who wanted to sell you an item behaved in a way that struck you as suspicious. The more the individual talked about the item, the more you felt uncomfortable and cautious. You had enough information to know that the item itself was worth buying, but you still hesitated because you had no information about the seller's motivation. Somehow the more the salesperson talked, the more you wanted the item, but the less you wanted to buy it from that particular individual. Even before deciding whether or not to make the purchase, you firmly decided you wouldn't do business with this person. Essentially, your decision was based on one thing: distrust.

Many of us encounter the same dilemma when we must decide whether to develop a relationship with someone. Although a person attempts to persuade us to get involved with them, we hesitate or avoid opportunities for doing so. While we want friendships with others, there is something about certain people that keeps us at a distance. How they behave and what they say tends to lower the level of trust we have in them. Their credibility becomes questionable, and often we are unwilling to take the risk of finding out if they are really trustworthy.

The foundation of developing credibility with others rests on the fact that your credibility always exists in the minds of others. What you think of yourself is only valid if others agree with your self-assessment. Our self-perceptions are not what others evaluate us by. We tend to judge our interactions based on our intentions, whereas others focus more on our actual behavior. When the behavior doesn't match the intention, people use what we actually said and did to evaluate our credibility.

For example, a college professor gives extremely difficult exams to her freshman students because she wants them to fail the first time they take her course. She thinks they are too soft and she wants them to toughen up so that they can survive in the "real" world (this is representative of a high B,C approach to teaching and testing). Her approach is based on how she was taught and what she believes is best for her students. In her opinion, the students and other faculty should admire her for this approach, but because she has such high drop-out and failure rates, people say negative things about her. Her credibility drops as a result of her insensitivity to what the students need to learn.

Unfortunately, while instructors like this are very knowledgeable in their content areas, they often cannot transmit their knowledge to the students and are therefore ineffective teachers. Students become close-minded and do not learn because they sense the instructor does not personally care about them and is not trustworthy. This sad situation is repeated in one form or another in countless schools, businesses, training programs, and organizations of all types—in fact, any place where human relationships are at work.

Just for a moment, do a quick exercise. Try to imagine how others perceive you; that is, "put the shoe on the other foot." Ask yourself, How much credibility do I have with others?

A Process for Developing Credibility Skills

A major way to improve your relationships with others is to increase the level of credibility you have with them. Credibility is best measured by the level of confidence others have in you. It is an indicator of how much they trust you and believe you can be relied upon to treat them fairly. Usually the level of respect and affection you receive from others is directly related to how much credibility you have developed with them.

Credibility is developed mostly through the use of positive attitudes and behaviors. Individuals who behave in a manner that consistently indicates they respect and care for others build their credibility levels higher than those individuals who do not behave in such a way. For instance, when President Nixon was caught telling lies about the Watergate break-in, he lost much credibility in the eyes of the American public. His behavior regarding the investigation and cover-up was interpreted as disrespect for the people whose interests he claimed to be representing. The more he insisted he was not a crook, the more the public believed that he was. The more he stated he was innocent, the more the American public lost faith in him. The trust factor had been broken.

One of the central purposes of this book is to describe how you can increase credibility with others through the use of certain skills. As mentioned in Chapter 10, a skill is an acquired behavior that you can consistently perform well in various situations. If a person can hammer a nail straight into a piece of wood nine times out of ten, then it can be said that the person has the skill of using a hammer; if an individual can only do it three times out of ten, then he or she not have the skill of hammering.

Without credibility we cannot establish, develop, or maintain our relationships. To improve our credibility, we must follow a process that will help us to develop three credibility-building skills:

1. Translating
2. Suspending
3. Style-shifting

Translating is the skill of knowing the differences between the four personal style dimensions well enough to be able to identify these differences when you encounter them in someone else's behavior. Without this knowledge, it is close to impossible to complete the next two phases.

Suspending is the skill of refraining from particular style behaviors that bother other people. Such style behaviors can prevent others from moving closer to you. For example, if you are very verbal, your talking could become a block for someone who prefers being nonverbal. Having the ability or self-control to suspend your desire to talk too much when around such a person would help them to feel more comfortable with you.

Style-shifting is the skill of demonstrating particular behaviors that fit other people's personal needs (even if they may not fit your own) so that other people feel more comfortable interacting with you. This requires the skills of translating and suspending to successfully match approaches and behaviors with particular style patterns as demonstrated by others.

To get a clearer understanding of how to use personal style theory in relationships, we'll explore each skill in the process of developing credibility with others. The first skill, translating, will be explained in this chapter. The skills of suspending and style-shifting will be discussed in Chapter 13, and Chapters 14 and 15, respectively.

When an individual enters the presence of others, they commonly seek to acquire information about him or to bring into play information about him already possessed....
Information about the individual helps to define the situation, enabling others to know in advance what he will expect of them and what they may expect of him. Informed in these ways, the others will know how best to act in order to call forth a desired response from him.
— Erving Goffman

Translating the Language of Personal Style

When two people with different personal styles hold a conversation, they may feel as if they were speaking to each other across a chasm or through a wall, understanding only vaguely what is being said to them and wondering why it is so difficult to get their own message across. The chasm or wall is not a figment of their imagination, but an obstacle that can be likened to the language barrier between people who speak different languages. And how people with different personal styles try to deal with this obstacle can be as diverse as how those who speak different languages try to get around the language barrier.

Communication difficulties block meaning and understanding between people, therefore blocking the mutual acceptance that must exist if people are to develop and maintain rewarding relationships. These difficulties can lead to misinterpretations that generate confusion and an overall misunderstanding of the intentions and concerns of another person. Parents and teenagers, in particular, tend to experience communication problems because they find it difficult to convey their thoughts and feelings in a way that is meaningful to each other. Without meaning to provide a bridge between them and to structure their verbal exchange, what begins as a discussion descends into confusion. Husbands and wives, employees and employers, students and teachers— any combination of people you can think of—may experience similar communication problems.

Ineffective communication usually results in frustration, and a relationship can severely suffer from the strain caused by misunderstanding. Credibility levels between people drop and distrust begins to build; instead of becoming more willing to cooperate with each other, people become less willing, and suspicion levels rise. Developing credibility with others therefore depends on how well you can "translate" what people are saying about themselves into information you can understand, so that you can respond to them in ways that they will understand. The skill of translating is a significant key to credibility, and having a clear understanding of how personal style differences influence relationships can help you develop this skill.

In human relations a little language goes further than a little of almost anything else. Whereas one language now often makes a wall, two can make a gate.

— Walter V. Kaulfers

Translating involves understanding the personal style "language" through which the speaker is communicating. People add personalized meanings to words to go along with what those words actually mean. This often confuses those who are listening, because they usually translate the words of the speaker into their understanding of the environment rather than first discovering what the words actually mean to the speaker.

For instance, what happens when Andy talks with Bill about renovating Bill's home? He communicates from an affective point of view, while Bill listens to Andy and judges what he is hearing from a behavioral frame of reference. Bill grows frustrated because Andy uses too many words to explain his ideas and doesn't get right to the point. Andy, in turn, is frustrated because no matter how expressive he is, he can't seem to influence Bill to agree with his new creative plan for developing Bill's house.

This frustration will only mount, and probably cause an argument, unless Andy can find a way to present his ideas in a way that Bill will understand. Taking Bill's personal style into consideration and accommodating that style as he speaks would help Andy do this. He would discover that he can get his message across to Bill by presenting facts and figures, by taking less time in the presentation, and by explaining to Bill how the changes would help Bill in his line of work.

Naturally you want to feel understood when you talk with others, just as they want to feel understood when they talk with you. When you understand another person, even if only during a few verbal exchanges, your credibility is increased, for the person feels you care. By understanding that person's personal style—and the values, needs, and fears associated with it—you then begin to develop a more accurate perception of how that person sees the world. Add this understanding to your other knowledge and skills regarding interpersonal communication and you can develop a fairly reliable system for "hearing" what other people are really saying. By comprehending what their messages mean to them and by demonstrating behaviors and attitudes that are appropriate for developing relationships, you will find that most individuals want to cooperate with you.

Reading and Assessing the Signs

If you have taken the PSI, you know your personal style pattern. Figuring out someone else's personal style pattern is not as easy. You could, of course, ask the person to fill out a PSI, or you could complete another PSI yourself, this time giving responses on how you perceive the person. But you don't always have time to do this, and you probably don't carry a stack of PSIs around with you anyway. So what can you do instead?

If, for whatever reason, you can't use a PSI, then you have to develop an educated guess about what that individual's personal style is. This is done by closely observing the individual's daily behavior patterns and then evaluating those patterns using criteria based upon personal style theory. Clearly, this isn't going to be possible unless you have already learned how to assess personal style characteristics and have practiced the technique.

The key to translating is learning how to read the signs that all individuals display. These signs are exhibited in our daily behavior patterns. We all nonverbally tell each other what our style preferences are. By observing how others approach and interact with the environment, we can start to gain some idea of what style pattern they might have. I say "might have" because we can never really know for sure.

Making decisions based upon the theoretical concepts of personal style theory is not difficult once you comprehend the main differences between the four dimensions. The criteria used to explain such differences were presented earlier in Chapter 7, in summary form, as we examined the personal style model. To make this task easier I have included the Personal Style Assessment Sheet (see Chart 12.1 on page 148). It provides you with the necessary information for assessing the personal styles of others.

The chart consists of 20 characteristics according to which you can assess someone's personal style. Each characteristic has been rated according to how it compares with each one of the personal style dimensions. This has been done using frequency ratings that indicate how often individuals with that predominant personal style dimension might tend to demonstrate that particular characteristic in their behavior pattern.

To see how this works, let's consider introversion, the first characteristic. Individuals with interpersonal styles tend to exhibit introverted behaviors more often (80-99%) than people with cognitive styles (50-79%). People with cognitive styles, in turn, are more introverted than people with behavioral styles (26-49%), while people with affective styles are least likely to behave in an introverted manner (0-25%).

Chart 12.1—The Personal Style Assessment Sheet

Frequency Characteristics	80-99% Most like:	50-79% Then like:	26-49% Next like:	0-25% Least like:
Introverted	I	C	B	A
Extroverted	A	B	C	I
People-Oriented	A	I	C	B
Task-Oriented	B	C	I	A
Quiet, Shy	I	B	C	A
Talkative	A	C	B	I
Action-Oriented	B	I	A	C
Analytical	C	A	B	I
Unemotional	B	C	A	I
Emotional	I	A	C	B
Wants Results	B	C	I	A
Perfectionistic	C	B	I	A
Likes Variety	A	B	I	C
Prefers Routine	C	I	B	A
Desires Harmony	I	A	C	B
Seeks Excitement	A	B	I	C
Acts Independently	B	A	I	C
Puts Others First	I	A	C	B
Attends to Details	C	I	B	A
Expects Respect	C	I	A	B

To evaluate an individual by using this sheet, you would read each characteristic and ask yourself how often, on average, the person you are rating exhibits this characteristic. You would then circle the letter of the dimension (B, C, I, A) that corresponds to the frequency with which you think the individual demonstrates that characteristic. For instance, using the characteristic "people-oriented" I might circle the "I" for someone who appears to be this way five to seven times out of ten (50%-79%). This would mean that even though the person is strongly oriented toward people, there is moderate task-orientation as well, whereas someone who was evaluated in the 80-99% category would have very little task-orientation.

Once you have rated the individual on each characteristic, look for the personal style dimension that seems most predominant. To determine this, add up the number of times you circled each letter (B, C, I, and A) so that you have four scores, one for each dimension. Rank the scores from high to low, recording the letter of the dimension along with its score. By looking at this ranking, you can decide how influential each dimension is. Follow this key:

Score	Influence
9-10	Strong
7-8	Moderate
1-6	Weak

Only use the dimensions (letters) that scored 7 or higher to determine the personal style pattern. For example, suppose your final assessment scores for one of your co-workers are as follows:

I-9, C-7, B-4, A-0

This would indicate that you perceive the person as strong in the interpersonal and cognitive dimensions, because these two scores amount to 7 or more. Since the "I" score is higher than the "C" score, the person may possess the style pattern known as Thoughtful. (If you have a copy of the *PSI In-Depth Interpretations Booklet*, you can look up this particular style pattern—or any of the other 20 patterns—to discover what strengths and weaknesses are characteristic of this pattern.)

Of course, trying to assess a person's style in this way is not easy. Individuals who have style flexibility (strength in three or four dimensions) will be the most difficult to evaluate because their behavior patterns tend to vary so much among the different dimensions. Observing them over a longer period of time and in different situations would increase your chances of evaluating them accurately.

Please remember that these criteria and frequencies should only be used as guidelines. Your evaluations are simply educated guesses based on how you perceive others interacting with their environment around them. It is unfortunate that our powers of observation tend to be so distorted by our own frames of reference, because this means we can't be sure that our assessment of someone's style has much accuracy. We may be reading the wrong signs or responding to the wrong signals.

Nevertheless, since we don't seem to be able to prevent ourselves from making judgments about other people's feelings and personalities, we might as well try to turn this natural human tendency to our advantage. We might just be pleasantly surprised by what we gain in the process. To achieve these advantages, though, we need to do more than try to guess at someone else's personal style—we need to act on the information as well. Doing this requires that we recognize how we are presently behaving toward others. In other words, we should get a good grip on ourselves first.

Chapter 13.
Get A Grip

The greatest of faults . . .
is to be conscious of none.

— Thomas Carlyle

Stop Blocking the Way

Road hogs are annoying. They don't seem to notice how they are straddling lanes on the highway and slowing down other traffic, nor do they appear to care about the chains of vehicles that form behind them on narrow country roads. They turn the virtue of driving slowly and carefully into a vice, and they seem oblivious to the needs of others. The same problems can occur with "style hogs"—people who unconsciously let the influence of their personal style dominate their attitudes and behaviors to such an extent that effective communication with others becomes difficult to maintain. They block other people out of the picture.

The way to avoid becoming a style hog is to develop the skill of "suspending." This is the second phase in the process of developing credibility. It involves learning to deliberately eliminate or suppress those behaviors that block others from developing a deeper relationship with us. I call this process suspending because it demands that we set aside any behavior that puts up a barrier that prevents others from getting closer to us. These behaviors are often perceived by others as evidence that we do not care to have a deeper relationship with them.

Suspending works best when it is tailored to the individual with whom you are interacting. What works well for one individual may not work well with another. To do this effectively requires an understanding of the other person's preferred style. For example, a co-worker with a strong cognitive style such as Connie's may enjoy talking intimately about personal matters when you go on a coffee break together. But a co-worker

151

like Bill may feel uncomfortable talking about his personal life because he is strongly influenced by the behavioral dimension. Sharing personal information with Connie will help to relax her and make her feel at ease with you, but to achieve the same effect with Bill, you would need to focus the conversation on work-related matters.

Those of you who possess strong style pattern flexibility may have a difficult time with suspending because you are often trying to suspend characteristics that are related to more than one style dimension. It is essential that you learn to identify when you are in one dimension or another. For instance, a person who is strong in the cognitive, interpersonal, and affective dimensions will shift between those dimensions frequently. This shifting also confuses others, for they are not sure what "side" of your personality will show up next.

Our ability to suspend style behaviors can be hindered by the typical barriers which each dimension produces. These tend to block the ease with which we can lay aside our natural preferences and try to adjust our behavior to fit the circumstances we find ourselves in. The rest of the chapter examines what these blocks are and how we can try to overcome their influence on us. Four blocks for each dimension are discussed. Please note these are typical blocks only. People who are strong in the same dimension will tend to suffer from the same blocks, but not necessarily to the same extent. Also, the influence of these blocks tends to be weakened by social conditioning and other forms of learning.

Any virtue carried to extreme can become a crime.

— **Alexandre Dumas**

Typical Behavioral Blocks

Bill is a very independent person and well able to take care of himself; he needs others far less than most individuals who are strong in the other dimensions. Yet other people need him, and sometimes he should take more responsibility for bending in ways that can meet the needs of others as well as his own. If individuals like Bill work at removing the following blocks, they can be of greater assistance to others. This, in turn, will help them to feel less isolated.

1. Let others live in your world.

Bill often keeps others at a distance because of his need for independence and freedom. He usually wants control of any decision-making process that will personally affect him. He likes to work alone and often spends much of his time focused on work tasks, which leaves him little time to socialize with others. Bill needs to be sensitive to the fact that this can create unnecessary concerns for others who are trying to relate to him on a more personal level. Not letting them do so may very well cost him, and them, much in the end.

For instance, as a father, Bill might spend long hours at work and come home only to go out into his backyard workshop and spend several hours building furniture. While a child who is strong in the behavioral dimension would not have too much difficulty with this lack of attention, a child who is strong in the cognitive dimension would probably feel rejected or uncared for, because he or she would want more intimacy than Bill is providing.

2. Pride goes before a fall.

Bill is strong-willed and determined in what he believes is right. He seldom varies in his opinion. He tends to have a high level of self-regard, which can cause stress for others. Very often he is sorry for making a mistake but is unwilling or unable to admit it because of his nonverbal orientation. Others interpret this behavior as pride, and he loses credibility in their eyes. Making whatever adjustment is needed to avoid repeating the mistake is Bill's way of taking care of the situation. But others do not realize this. Bill needs to be aware that his pattern of behavior may end up hurting others because his orientation to task is much stronger than his sensitivity to people. It can lead him to appear prideful and hard-hearted to others even when this may not really be the case.

There are several reasons why Bill finds it difficult to admit that he has been wrong and to apologize for mistakes he has made. First, he does not tend to make many mistakes. Second, he perceives apologizing as a sign of submission or defeat that could possibly be used against him at a later time. Admitting his shortcomings will not make him weak, despite what he thinks. Instead, it will help others to see that he cares as much about them as he does about himself.

When Bill refuses to shift his style for others, and this can occur frequently, other people suffer. He should remember others are not as "tough" as he is and that they often need more care and attention than he naturally feels comfortable giving. To improve his relationships with others, he could "soften up" to some extent and let them know that he too can be sensitive toward people. If you are in the company of a person with a strong behavioral style such as Bill's, lower your expectations a little. Don't expect this particular person to be as warm, sociable, and humble as you may be. Such expectations reveal the desire to change the natural tendencies of an individual and merely leads to stress and resentment.

3. Sharing yourself will not make you weak.

Bill believes talking about situations seldom solves anything and that action is the best cure for all problems. Being oriented toward independence, he firmly believes that it is each individual's responsibility to solve his or her own problems. Hence, he is less likely to seek counseling, medical treatment, or other kinds of assistance than people with other personal styles. While this confidence in his own ability may be noble, it can also lead others to believe he doesn't trust them or care enough to let them help him.

Bill also does not like sharing personal feelings and thoughts. The more he is hurting inside, the more he will be apt to withdraw and isolate himself. He usually takes care of his needs first and later returns to talk with others about situations they are having trouble with. He also tends to be more verbal when he feels good about himself and when others are discussing work-related subjects. This preoccupation with his own agenda and this withholding of personal feelings can give others the impression that Bill is aloof and does not care—when often he really does.

4. Learn to shift your style to fit other's needs.

One strength Bill has as an individual is that he can be very immovable in his opinions and beliefs. He is a person who is sure about what it is he wants to do and what it is you can do for him. This personal quality is of great importance in many different areas of life, such as business and school. Yet in social relationships, it may prove to be the one characteristic to which others have the most difficulty adjusting. This occurs because he is so firm in his beliefs and attitudes that in his eyes there is little chance that someone else who disagrees with him is right.

While Bill can successfully take care of himself, we should recognize that he may not be good at understanding what others need, think, or feel. This lack of understanding can prevent his overcoming shallow relationships with others who want to be closer to him. While they may have a strong respect for what he has accomplished in his life, they could also end up viewing him as the stranger whom they once wanted to get to know.

Typical Cognitive Blocks

Those of you who are strong in this dimension care about others and life very much, yet your methods of showing your caring to others often push them away, which is exactly the opposite of what you want to accomplish. If you develop your ability to love others in ways that are important to them, you will find the caring and respect that you want to receive. The following suggestions will help you in doing so.

1. Anger will not bring you respect.

Connie has a high need for respect. When others reject her opinion or advice, she usually gets angry and upset. By getting angry and overreacting in other negative ways, she loses credibility with those whom she is trying to influence. This anger is a block that can cost her much more than she realizes. She says that she doesn't care about what people think or say, but the truth of the matter is that Connie cares very much, which is why she is so angry in the first place. People seldom get upset about things that are not important to them.

2. Control yourself rather than other people.

Connie also has a tendency to try to control others. This can occur because of her strong need for safety and intimacy. As a high-cognitive parent, for example, she will likely be overprotective of her children because she has a strong need to know they're safe and secure. This need can become destructive in the relationship if she does not control it and if she becomes obsessive in keeping tight limits on the child.

This particular block most often occurs in verbal attempts to make others do what she thinks they should be doing. Connie can be manipulative in verbally trying to convince others that her way is the right way. When she does this, she often comes across as dogmatic and insensitive to others, which makes them feel alienated. Connie can develop more credibility and be more effective in helping others if she takes more responsibility for her behavior rather than tries to control what other people do.

155

3. Criticize tasks, not people.

Connie is a perfectionist and, therefore, usually tends to be an advice-giver. She believes telling others what is wrong with them actually helps them solve their problems. As a boss, she might say to an employee, "That's not the way you talk to someone on the phone. Let me show you how to do it." While this approach may get the message across that the employee is inappropriately using the phone, it can also leave the individual feeling discouraged. Being "right" is effective in developing credibility only if Connie is also being sensitive to the other person's needs.

This problem is caused in part by Connie's tendency to freely verbalize what she thinks. She is also naturally more sensitive to tasks than to people. She often tends to blame others for not completing tasks the "right" way. When this happens, she can come across as being critical. For example, Connie might say to an employee after overhearing a telephone conversation, "I don't understand why you say such stupid things over the phone." This leaves the employee feeling attacked and believing Connie thinks he or she is stupid. This kind of criticism does not encourage the employee to want to learn a better way of making a phone call.

4. Think and talk less; listen and do more.

Another cognitive block that hinders Connie's success in developing relationships is her tendency to analyze and verbalize instead of taking action. In relationships, there is definitely a time to turn off the computer upstairs (your brain), stop talking, and listen. Connie's problem is that she tends to "overthink" while she is talking; she actually is trying to sort out what is in her mind as she talks, and consequently often spends more time thinking about what she is going to say than listening to someone else talk. Learning how to listen attentively to what others have to say before reacting with her own "agenda" could strongly reduce stress in her relationships.

Sometimes this kind of "overthinking" results in worrying about every little detail. As a result, people with strong cognitive styles like Connie can have difficulty making decisions. Because Connie's high need for respect pressures her to avoid mistakes, often she doesn't act in enough time and a mistake is made. Instead of gathering the information necessary for the decision and acting on it, people like Connie tend to analyze every possible course of action and balk at actually taking any of them.

Typical Interpersonal Blocks

Individuals who are strong in the interpersonal dimension usually need to be more assertive in their daily interactions. Their non-assertive approach to life can actually become a serious obstacle for others who wish to develop relationships with them. If you are a person with a strong interpersonal style like Isabella's, then the following suggestions should be of assistance to you.

1. Stand up for what you believe is right.

A major block for Isabella is her passive behavior. Being naturally humble can be beneficial in many situations, but it can also keep others from really getting to know what is important to her. If she wants a more "equal" relationship with others, then she has to be willing to take the risk of sharing herself with them. While they won't always agree with her, they will respect her more for standing up for what she believes in.

Learning to be more assertive will be difficult for Isabella because she has such a strong need for harmony as well as a large fear of conflict. The thought of standing up and stating what is important to her scares Isabella, for she is afraid someone may become angry with her for doing so. This fear has to be overcome if she is to develop self-esteem.

2. If you can't say it, write it down.

Because Isabella tends not to verbalize, sharing feelings with others, especially feelings about personal issues, is often difficult . Her need for harmony is so strong that when she is put on the spot, she often finds her mind goes blank and she chokes with emotion. She has trouble expressing her thoughts and feelings because she is more preoccupied with what others are saying and feeling.

Isabella could try removing this particular block by writing down what she wants to say to someone before trying to say it. Once she has done this, she can either give this piece of paper to the person or verbalize the words aloud to herself. This allows her time to think of what it is she really wants to say.

3. Let others take care of themselves.

Another block that can hinder relationships is Isabella's high need to nurture others. While some individuals may appreciate her efforts to care for them, others may have different needs and either ignore or mis-understand her intentions. Also, some people may perceive her over-caring for them as a sign of disrespect for their ability to take care of themselves, and they may resent her for trying to "parent" them with her concerns. This is especially true when Isabella starts to "overcare" for her teenage children.

This type of behavior pattern results from Isabella's strong need to feel appreciated and to love others. A key way for her to gain this appre-ciation is for her to get involved in others' lives. She does this naturally by doing things for people. This is very noble, and it is a good way for Isabella to show her concern for others as long as it does not become her identity. She should not want her value as a person to be determined by what she does for others, nor should she let her strong need to nurture control her behavior toward others in such a way that it costs her cred-ibility with them. Isabella would improve her relationships if she was as caring toward herself as she is toward others.

4. There's a time and place for stubbornness, but this is not it.

Isabella is a very warm and loving person who often thinks less of herself than she does of others, but when she has been wronged or feels strongly about an issue, she can become extremely stubborn. She sends others nonverbal messages that convey how really upset she is. Unfor-tunately, others can perceive these messages as signs of passive aggres-siveness. For example, she does not say anything; she just stands her ground silently, even sullenly. When this occurs, others are less apt to cooperate with her. Even if they recognize her nonverbal messages, these people still may not know why she is upset with them.

Expressing her feelings overtly is a far more effective method for Isabella than going "on strike," for this approach gets her point across sooner and more accurately. While she thinks others understand her nonverbal communication, they are more likely ignoring her or misread-ing the message. Although there is a risk that others may not change, by sharing her feelings and opinions she is at least letting people know that she is not trying to punish them. Even if sullen silence periodically works for her, withdrawing from others will not gain her any credibility with them in the long run. Others will become tired of being shut out just as quickly as she will become tired of what they do to irritate her. By standing her ground and communicating her opinions and feelings, she will have a better chance of obtaining the appreciation she needs than she will have by remaining stubborn.

Typical Affective Blocks

People who want to develop a closer relationship with Andy often wonder, Is he reliable? He seems like he is, and he talks like he is, but when the pressure is on, where is he? If you are high in the affective dimension, then improving yourself in the following areas of difficulty can help you develop your credibility.

1. Be on time because you care.

One common frustration others may experience with Andy is his lack of attention to time. He is so people-oriented and creative that he loves to stop and talk with people or to dream up new ideas, which often distracts him from his responsibilities. He is often late for appointments and occasionally forgets them altogether. This kind of behavior often leads others to think he doesn't care about them and is self-centered. Andy should keep his appointments, or not make them. If he is going to be late or has a change of plans, he should consider calling ahead, before the appointment time passes, to let others know about it.

2. Stay out of debt.

Of the four dimensions, the affective dimension has the most influence on an individual's need for pleasure. Andy likes to indulge—to play, to be active, and to entertain—and this can sometimes cost more money than he can afford. Activities like going to parties or eating out regularly can be expensive and can slide him into financial difficulties all too easily. Going into debt usually doesn't scare him as much as it would scare Isabella. Being naturally optimistic, he believes he can wriggle out of debt with a little creative thinking and financing. Too often this only slides him into deeper financial trouble and causes strain on others who have to live or work with him.

The fact that Andy cannot pay for something doesn't always slow him down, as he is an impulsive decision-maker when it comes to doing almost everything. He is generous with his money and possessions because he needs the acceptance of others, which he receives by spending money and loaning possessions. For a good example of this, consider Andy when he was a 10-year old who just had to have that new bike with all the bells and whistles on it. He swore to his father he would take care of the bike, but he let every kid on the block ride it; then he left it abandoned in the street while playing baseball, only to have it stolen when he wasn't looking.

159

3. It's essential that you finish what you start.

Andy has so many ideas and interests that he is constantly starting one project after another—and seldom finishing any of them. It's not that he is insincere about completing the tasks, it's just that he is easily misled by other interests. If Andy made fewer commitments and followed through on those already made, he would be perceived and recognized for his accomplishments. Rather than overbooking, he needs to learn to say no to others, for their sake as well as his own. When he promises more than he can deliver, it severely diminishes his level of credibility with others. Instead of getting the acceptance he wants from others, he often ends up losing it.

4. Work is not a dirty word.

While play is at the top of Andy's list of things to do, work is near or at the bottom. Since Andy is people-oriented and focused on pleasure, he would much rather use his time and energy doing things that are fun. When work includes meeting different people and discussing their interests, as does a sales position in a sporting goods store, then work is often quite fulfilling for people like Andy. When variety and involvement with people are lacking, then Andy's motivation sags and he easily becomes bored and loses interest.

Maintaining sustained effort can be difficult for Andy because he tends to lack the stamina and persistence needed to achieve projects that become arduous or tedious. If others must depend on Andy to complete work tasks and he leaves the tasks half-finished because he finds them boring, then he is placing an unfair burden upon his co-workers, which will make him very unpopular. This could also affect his family life. For example, Andy's wife may admire him partly because he is kind and sensitive to people, but if he consistently starts jobs and quits them because he's bored, he could put the family into financial difficulties that she may find difficult to forgive him for.

We succeed in enterprises that demand
the positive qualities we possess, but we excel
in those that can also make use of our defects.

— Alexis de Tocqueville

Getting Ready to Style-Shift

Learning how to recognize the behaviors or attitudes in yourself that keep you from moving forward and then learning how to overcome their influence are important steps. You may find that some of these blocks are obstinate and require plenty of attention before their influence weakens, but with practice you can prevent these attitudes from poisoning your relationships with other people. The way forward requires that you develop control over your personal style rather than simply letting it control you.

What about other people and their blocks, though? How do you go about developing credibility with others who may not be as self-aware or as self-controlled as you? How can you learn to adjust to other people's styles of behavior? How should you tackle "style hogs" when you encounter them? How can you learn to shift from your naturally preferred style into a style that is more appropriate to specific situations? The next chapter explores the answers to such questions by discussing the technique called "style-shifting."

Chapter 14.
Shift for a Change

Change is not . . . the transformation of one-self into something entirely different, but rather its expansion into a more vivid realization of what we already are.
The urge toward change is invariably accompanied by the fear of changing. To stand still requires the courage to defend what you now are; to risk change requires the still greater courage of discovering what you might become.

— Richard Grossman

Why Must I Be the One to Change?

Have you ever been in an unstable relationship that just wasn't getting any better? Most of us have, at one time or another. Your frustration with the other person's behavior can often lead you to become defensive, unfriendly, and sometimes even aggressive toward the individual. Still, deep down inside, you don't want this frustration to continue and build up into even stronger emotions. So what can you do to stop it? The answer is, you can change how you behave toward the person even if that individual doesn't choose to change the way he or she is behaving toward you.

When I teach this concept in my classes and seminars, one question repeatedly comes up: "Why do I have to be the one to change?" My answer is always the same: "If one of you doesn't change, the relationship won't improve." I tell people that if they don't want their relationships to improve, then by all means they should continue behaving in their usual way. But I also inform them that close relationships rarely remain static—

they tend to either get better or get worse. They don't improve without sacrifice and effort, and one person doing this is better than nobody doing it.

The key to effective change is knowing how to change in such a way that you do not stop being yourself. You can learn to demonstrate new behaviors that are rewarding for both you and the other person. Assertiveness training and many other self-development programs are built upon principles such as this one.

However important principles are, though, it is worth remembering that, as Oscar Wilde said, "it is personalities, not principles that move the age." He was discussing history here, but the same is true of relationships. People, not ideas, are what make relationships better. Everyday each one of us makes some sort of decision regarding the relationships we have. Do we put more or less effort into the relationship? Some associations we choose to develop, while others we let deteriorate. Still, once you have identified relationships you would like to improve, it is the combination of knowledge, skills and determination that bring the best results.

When such knowledge and skills are consistently applied to relationships, your credibility with people is more likely to increase. I say "more likely" because other people still have a will of their own, and if people choose not to let the relationship improve, there is little that knowledge and skills will do to change their minds. Yet, these individuals are the exception rather than the rule. Most people will respond in a more positive manner when approached in the way that best fits their style and needs. This type of approach is known as "style-shifting."

Style-Shifting Increases Credibility

When we are driving a car, we use a gearshift to shift from one gear to another. This helps to reduce the strain on the transmission when the vehicle is moving slowly or traveling uphill. People are not machines, of course, but the technique of style-shifting is similar to shifting gears in a car because it involves shifting our styles to match the needs of the environment we find ourselves in. When we style-shift, we try to switch into a more appropriate gear. What makes one gear more appropriate than another is how well the behaviors we demonstrate fit the people, situations, and tasks we are trying to deal with.

When interacting with a strong cognitive person such as Connie, for example, I would want to be aware of what behaviors fit cognitive patterns of behavior. I would want to tell Connie details and give her time to think or analyze the information before I asked her for an opinion. On the other hand, in an emergency situation, acting in a behavioral style might be more suitable because I would need to make quick decisions and be action-oriented. If I were attempting to sell door-to-door, I would try to adopt a noticeably positive attitude, to become enthusiastic and people-oriented, and in so doing, draw upon behaviors typical of affective styles.

Style-shifting is the third step in developing credibility with others, but it actually builds upon the other two steps. Style-shifting involves understanding what other styles and situations require (translating), keeping your style under control (suspending), and then shifting your behavior in such a way that you make others feel more understood and comfortable when interacting with you. For instance, let's say Isabella is working as a secretary for Bill. It would be to her advantage if she quickly completed her work, didn't question her assignments, and was verbally direct and to the point when she did not agree with something she was asked to do. All of these characteristics tend to fit Bill's style more than Isabella's. If Isabella demonstrated these sorts of behaviors when interacting with Bill (although not excessively or slavishly), Bill would perceive her as an efficient secretary.

While style-shifting requires you to develop each of your personal style dimensions to the limit of their potential, it does not mean you should try to be someone you are not. It simply suggests that you "move" into the most appropriate pattern of behavior for the situation and people involved. While this is not always possible, it can be learned, and with practice you can improve, if not perfect, the skill areas related to your weaker dimensions.

The exciting thing about learning to style-shift is that in the process of shifting you can also develop skill areas in which you are weak. For instance, I am weakest in the behavioral dimension. But through practice I have become much more effective when I interact with people who have behavioral styles. In order to do this, I have to suspend the influence of my strong cognitive dimension and behave more like a person with a behavioral style when I am around them. Instead of providing them with details in which they are not interested, I get to the point quickly and state the facts. I am also polite, but not as friendly toward them as I would be toward others, for they are not as comfortable with that sort of behavior. Doing this type of shifting has raised my credibility with people who have behavioral styles, because I am operating more like they would.

Style-shifting is also important when you are in situations that demand that you shift your style to fit the particular circumstances of the situation. For example, Isabella is normally shy and easily embarrassed by having to talk in public, yet there are times when doing so could be rewarding and beneficial for others, such as at awards ceremonies or fund-raising events. By helping other people in these sorts of situations, Isabella receives appreciation from others, which meets an important need of hers. By challenging herself to go beyond her natural limitations, she gains more than if she chooses not to shift. The key element here is being aware of what the situation calls for and attempting to shift your style to fit the circumstances as well as you possibly can. How to determine which approaches might work best with each of the personal style dimensions will be discussed later in this chapter.

Style-Shifting Because You Care

If your relationships are to develop and mature, it is essential that you attempt to see the world as others do and then shift your behavior pattern to fit theirs as often as possible. Why? So that they feel cared for. Connie might do this for her husband, Andy, by going out with him and doing something he enjoys, such as playing miniature golf, even though she may think it is a complete waste of time and money. She must also allow him to teach her how to have fun while they are out together. For her to go and suffer through the experience will only cause resentment and frustration for both individuals. This will defeat the purpose of going out together in the first place.

As was mentioned in Chapter 8, when personal style dimensions clash, individuals can find themselves in situations where there is a loss of credibility and they do not want to be around each other. They attribute the other person's behavior to spitefulness when often the other person is behaving according to his or her style. This style is part of the fabric of that person's self, and would remain constant regardless of companion or company. For example, when Andy goes to play miniature golf, he is usually loud and boisterous with everyone around him. He doesn't behave this way just because Connie has decided to join him for the evening. But if she didn't know this, she might think he was showing off, which could make her feel embarrassed and angry at him.

Knowing that Andy's behavior is greatly influenced by his personal style can help Connie avoid overpersonalizing or overreacting to Andy's particular way of playing miniature golf. Also, if Connie realizes that her style is often task-oriented, then perhaps she could learn how to have more fun by trying to shift Andy's style. Andy, in turn, could learn from her how to be more task-oriented when he needs to be instead of relying on his creativity and self-expression, which aren't always appropriate to the situation.

Learning about another person's style and what he or she needs is an excellent way to show that you care for that person. Shifting your behaviors to better fit his or her needs will greatly increase your credibility. In turn, it's also an excellent way to expand your abilities and skills. Regardless of what your particular style is, you can improve your control over each of the dimensions through knowledge and practice if you care enough to try.

Guidelines for Improving Your Effectiveness[*]

Style-shifting is not difficult to accomplish when you adopt the perspective provided by personal style theory and try to apply the knowledge you have gained about the four different dimensions of personal style. To assist you in learning how to go about applying this information, let's examine some guidelines.

1. Assess the style of the other person.
We have previously discussed how to assess other people's behavior patterns. By noting how consistently people behave according to the criteria specified in the Personal Style Model, you can begin to get an understanding of what their personal styles might be (see Chart 14.1 on page 168). If their behavior is very consistent over time and in different situations, then they most likely are high in just one of the dimensions. If they are quite varied in how they tend to approach and interact with the environment, then most likely they are style-flexible or simply shifting between several dimensions.

[*]Adapted from page 14 of the Personal Style Indicator.

2. Select appropriate style behaviors that fit the individual's primary style dimensions.

Most of us like to be treated as we tend to treat others. If you determine that a certain individual's behavior pattern is primarily task-oriented and nonverbal, then try behaving toward the individual in that way.

Chart 14.1—Assessment Criteria				
	Behavioral	**Cognitive**	**Interpersonal**	**Affective**
Extroverted	Yes	No	No	Yes
Introverted	No	Yes	Yes	No
Nonverbal	Yes	No	Yes	No
Verbal	No	Yes	No	Yes
Task-Oriented	Yes	Yes	No	No
People-Oriented	No	No	Yes	Yes

Most likely the individual will prefer action rather than talk. On the other hand, if an individual is introverted and people-oriented, then attempt to demonstrate behaviors that are sensitive and thoughtful, and allow the person to have his or her personal space. People feel more secure with individuals who perceive and interact as they do, and less sure of those who behave differently.

Again, it should be stressed here that if you do not have a good working knowledge of personal style differences, then trying to accomplish style-shifting will not be easy. It may not be sensible for you to even try. Time might be better spent on becoming more familiar with the characteristics of each dimension. Learning what makes each of the style dimensions unique in its influence on human behavior is really the foundation for building more effective relationships with others.

3. Implement your new style behaviors with the person.

Assertiveness is the key to being successful here. Having the confidence and courage to attempt to style-shift with others who are different from you allows you to try new behaviors. Keep your expectations realistic. When you first start, don't expect that everything will automatically work out. Look for opportunities to try out new behaviors rather than attempting to behave in a personal style dimension that *isn't you* for an extended period of time. Be especially careful with those dimensions in which you are naturally weak.

4. Observe and evaluate the impact of the behaviors on the other person.

When you are applying new behaviors, watch to see what impact they have on the other person. If the effect seems positive, then continue with the new behaviors; but if the result seems negative, then leave these new behaviors and discuss them with a mutual friend to assess what might be going wrong. Remember that the purpose of style-shifting is to develop better relationships with others, not to antagonize them.

As you are observing the process, ask yourself, "Is this behavior or approach working?" Attempt to assess why it is or isn't successful. If not successful, the reason could be that the person's style is not what you assume it to be or that they attempted to shift styles when you changed your behavior.

Record your observations and look for patterns that the other person displays on a regular basis in similar situations. For example, does the person tend to behave in a particular style whenever you go out for dinner? If so, then try to develop patterns of behavior that might work when you go out to eat with the person, but don't necessarily use those same behaviors at other times.

5. Reassess the results, make adjustments, and repeat the process as often as necessary.

Style-shifting is a process of trial and error. If at first you do not succeed, try, try again. Over time, things will begin to click into place as you consistently shift to fit that person's particular style. Style-shifting is also hard work. Improved relationships are not built in a day. You have to make a commitment to continue to work on style-shifting regardless of what others do in return. So often when we attempt some new behavior or attitude with others, they respond to us in an undesirable manner. When this happens, our first response is to stop the new behavior and to give up on trying to make a difference. What is more productive is to continue the new behavior for an extended period of time to determine how effective it can be with a particular individual.

It Takes Practice

These guidelines form a cycle of steps for style-shifting that can help you improve your relationships with others. Although I have seen almost immediate results many times, usually a length of time is needed for someone to become proficient at it and before the other individual will respond positively. Patience and persistence are required before results begin to appear. This is especially true with individuals with whom you already have long-established relationships. Since they are familiar with you behaving in certain characteristic ways, any style-shifting you do may confuse them.

A very good example of this is the relationship I have with my daughter, Pam, who is now 20. Until she reached the age of 11, I had little awareness that she had a style that was different from mine. This is not to say that I did not realize she was different from me in many ways, rather that I didn't understand who she really was. She met none of the expectations I had for my first-born child. I had expected a warm, affectionate little girl who would follow her parents everywhere. She, in turn, was extremely independent from the very beginning, and preferred not to be held or cuddled.

After she was three, we started to realize she thought of us simply as "the hired help" and that she was often irritated with us for getting in her way. Things did not improve much as she grew older. Even though she was a good child and did not cause trouble, there was still something missing for me, which I could not understand. She too sometimes wondered why she had to end up with a father like me.

As I learned more about personal styles, I suddenly saw for the first time who Pam really was. She is strong in the behavioral and interpersonal dimensions, moderate in the affective, and low in the cognitive dimension. Being strong in the cognitive and affective dimensions, I was very verbal, while Pam was very action-oriented. The more I talked to Pam, the less she liked it. The less she talked to me, the more rejected I felt. She had no use for organization, structure, or safety—all of which I strongly forced upon her. I did not believe that she, as a young child, could decide matters for herself. From her behavioral point of view, how could I possibly know what was best for her?

When Pam was 12, the rebellion came, and it was a good thing that my wife Denise and I had learned enough about styles to shift our approaches (although not our values or standards) to better fit her style. In style-shifting, I became much less affectionate toward her, came straight to the point when I talked with her, stopped debating with her about why she could not do something, and started treating her as if she were two years older. Previously when I disciplined her, I would limit her responsibilities and freedoms. Her reaction to this approach was to become bored or start to rebel. But when I shifted, I increased her freedom and increased her responsibilities, even when disciplining her. She, in turn, excelled not only at home but also at school. While Pam deserves all the credit for the results she has achieved, style-shifting played an important part in the process.

Now that she is married and working as an interior designer, we have a great relationship. She has learned about my style and is working on improving in several areas that are important to me—such as asking my advice about something she is considering doing and being more affectionate toward me, both of which do not come easily for people who have behavioral styles. It is taking time for us to build a better relationship, but it has been worth waiting for. She now gets more of her needs met, and so do I. This makes us both more motivated to work even harder at the style-shifting process. Nothing that is worth anything comes quickly, and all too often in this age of fast foods and quick-fix tools, we lose sight of what is most important in human relationships: giving of ourselves so that the other person is satisfied and striving to achieve lasting solutions.

Chapter 15.
The Secret of Success

If there is any secret of success, it lies in the ability to get the other person's point of view and see things from his angle as well as from your own.

— Henry Ford

How to Shift Your Style

Understanding the guidelines for style-shifting is one thing; knowing what to do with them is another. The most fundamental thing to remember is that *most people prefer to be treated in a manner similar to how they treat others.* This is the secret to successful style-shifting. By watching how people relate to others, you can pick up tips on how they like to be treated. For example, individuals who are high in a particular dimension tend to enjoy being around others who are also strong in that dimension. If you can shift into a pattern similar to theirs, they will react in a more positive manner than if you shift into a style pattern that is quite different from theirs.

To assist you with the style-shifting process, the remainder of this chapter looks at each one of the four style dimensions. Each section covers one dimension and provides you with basic information on individuals who are predominantly strong in that dimension, including how the dimension relates to the personal style assessment criteria and personal needs. To illustrate how you might use this information to style-shift, I will explain how I would personally shift my style to better fit the needs of our four fictional characters: Bill, Connie, Isabella and Andy. For easy reference, the basic characteristics of each dimension are presented in Chart 15.1 through 15.4, at the conclusion of this chapter.

Shifting With Bill

Once I have assessed Bill's style as being predominantly behavioral, I need to concentrate on what is characteristic about individuals who demonstrate this personal style. This involves taking into consideration that Bill's needs are strongest in the areas of *challenge*, *freedom*, and *achievement*.

First, I should remember that these individuals are usually *extroverted*. This means that Bill prefers to initiate action in the environment rather than react to it. As much as possible, I should allow him to be the leader and to set the course in whatever we are attempting to do. When I do not like what he is doing, I should confront him with it very directly and confidently, presenting the facts and stating why I do not approve.

Second, Bill is *action-oriented* toward tasks. This means Bill focuses more on obtaining results than on the process of ensuring quality. He doesn't really care how something is done as long as it is done quickly and efficiently. The more I can help Bill achieve what he wants to achieve, the better I will impress him as a person worth his consideration.

Third, Bill is *nonverbal*. I want to keep in mind that Bill is not a talker. He is not one to just sit around and "shoot the breeze." He says what he means and means what he says. He is generally not interested in more discussion than the situation calls for. He prefers conversations that get to the point and focus on solving problems.

With this knowledge clearly in mind, I would approach Bill from a task perspective rather than from a people perspective. In other words, I would not try to be overly friendly or intimate with Bill without his initiating this. I would keep focusing on tasks and objectives rather than on personal opinions and feelings. I would ask him how he would like to see things occur.

If I needed to express my point of view, I would use as few words as possible. I would also stand my ground with Bill. I would not let him intimidate me into thinking what he is thinking. I would not waste time when interacting with Bill, as he is more conscious of time than most people. I also would not tell him I was going to attempt to do something unless I knew for sure I could achieve it.

Shifting With Connie

Knowing that Connie is especially strong in the cognitive dimension, I should remember when interacting with her that she is predominantly task-oriented, verbal, and introverted. I should also keep in mind that her strongest needs are for *safety, respect,* and *intimacy.*

Since Connie is *introverted,* I must remember she is highly sensitive to environmental stimuli. This means she experiences stress from environmental stimuli more easily than individuals who are extroverted. I should be aware of how much more introverted she is in comparison to me, and try to shift in her direction for this particular factor as much as possible. Being too extroverted when around Connie may simply turn her off. For example, if we went out to dinner, I would want to keep extroverted behavior to a minimum when at the table with her. Talking too loudly during our conversation or inviting others over to join us might tend to upset her.

I also would want to pay close attention to Connie's *orientation* toward tasks. I would remember that people with cognitive styles are perfectionists and prefer organization. If I could help her to achieve quality results, she would react to me in a positive way. If I invited her over to my house to work on a project, I would be wise to clean the house up first and be sure that I was prepared to start work when she arrived.

Finally, I should take into consideration that Connie is *verbal.* I would need to learn how to listen to Connie and how to debate on those topics that she thinks are important. If she is strongly interested in history, I might ask her opinion about a certain period in history or perhaps a famous person from the past. I would expect her to be somewhat opinionated about what she discusses and would be prepared for her to dominate the conversation. I would also need to know that when Connie is upset she becomes either critical of others or stops talking and becomes angry. When she is not talking to me, I would want to check with her to ensure she is not upset with me about something.

Based on this information about people with cognitive styles, I would tend to spend more time with Connie on a one-to-one basis, rather than in a group. This would meet her need for intimacy better. People who have cognitive styles prefer private discussions of a personal nature over regular chitchat. I would listen to what she had to say carefully and ask questions about why she believed what she did. This would make her feel important and respected.

I would overlook (to a point) her criticism of others and her complaints about the world in general. People with cognitive styles have high expectations that often are not met by others, and as a result, disappointment and anger are common emotions for these people. I would have to understand her need to vent her feelings during conversations and have to learn not to personalize her feelings. If I wanted her to do something for me, I would give her very clear and detailed information on how I wanted it done, and by when. I would also not expect her to do too many things at once, as this could create stress for her.

Shifting With Isabella

People with interpersonal styles are most often nonverbal, people-oriented, and introverted. Their strongest needs are for *security*, *appreciation* and *love*.

People who are strongest in the interpersonal dimension are very *introverted* toward people, which simply means they are shy. Their shyness does not interfere with their ability to be sensitive or caring toward others. They often put others before themselves, and when focused on helping others in need, they tolerate short-term negative response to their actions. Although they tend to be *people-oriented*, they can easily become upset by negative opinions, feelings, and behaviors that are continually directed toward them.

Because people with interpersonal styles are *nonverbal*, they usually do not express their concerns to others because they do not want to be a bother to anyone. They are most verbal when they are happy and usually stop talking when under stress or when around hostile individuals. They let their actions speak for themselves and tend to judge others by how they treat people rather than by what they say.

Knowing that Isabella is strong in the interpersonal dimension would help me to be more sensitive to her need for appreciation. When she does something for me, I would especially want to let her know that I am grateful for what she has done. In doing so, I would also want to remember that since she tends to be nonverbal, she would probably be uncomfortable with too much verbal praise. In this particular situation, a simple thank-you when no one else is listening might be best, or perhaps a card expressing my appreciation would be most acceptable.

Since Isabella is predominantly people-oriented, I would want to do things for her and with her. For example, because she often goes out of her way to do things for other people, I would want to look for opportunities where I might do the same for her. People who possess interpersonal styles don't forget those who help them. I would also want to do things with Isabella that she enjoys doing. Often these activities would not be my first choice, but she would feel appreciated if I chose to spend my time doing them with her anyway. For example, if she liked to bake, my sitting in the kitchen and talking with her as she does so would mean a lot to her.

If Isabella were upset about something, I would need to let her have time to think about what she wanted to say. Knowing that people with interpersonal styles do not respond well verbally when under pressure, I would need to allow her more time to formulate her responses to me. I also would want to listen closely to how she felt about things. Listening is very important to those who are strong in the interpersonal dimension.

Shifting With Andy

Andy, like all people with affective styles, prefers to talk. He is much more people-oriented than he is task-oriented. He is strongly extroverted in his approach to the environment. He needs *attention*, *acceptance*, and *recognition* more than anything else.

Being strongly extroverted *toward people* (especially when in groups), the more people Andy can interact with, the better. He is very verbal and likes to talk with people in person and over the phone. His need for attention drives him to place himself in situations where he can be seen and attended to by as many others as possible. For this reason, he tends to work better in groups than alone. Being alone feels like punishment for people with affective styles.

Since Andy is so *people-oriented*, he spends most of his energy working on influencing others. His need for recognition leads him to hold back his best efforts unless he's sure he can receive some kind of praise for them. He often does his best work when the most pressure is on and others are expecting him to fail. He is motivated to gain other people's recognition. For instance, during regular practice sessions, this sort of player does not put out much effort when the coach starts yelling at him

177

to increase his performance. Yet, during the game, because the crowds and the media are watching him, he will make the superb catch that wins the game.

If I needed to shift my style toward Andy, I would want to approach him from my affective dimension. This means that I would want to do amusing or exciting things with him, tell him jokes, phone him often, and try not to put restrictions on him or our relationship. I would also want to acknowledge his talents and praise him for things he can do well. Doing this in front of others would be best. I would give him praise for his creative abilities and ideas rather than point out his faults. I would not expect of him to be highly reliable, especially in matters related to time and everyday tasks. Whatever it is that he is attempting to do, he will probably be late or slow in getting it done. My getting angry at him will not make him speed up, but it could so discourage him that he would stop putting out any effort.

A Final Word of Caution

While I want you to be able to directly apply this information about style-shifting in your lives, it is extremely important that you apply it in a respectful way when interacting with others. Remember, your credibility with others is determined by how you behave. As stated previously, personal style assessment and style-shifting are not the answers to all of life's problems. Using personal style concepts can greatly improve relationships, but other factors are just as important to consider when working on your associations with others. Relationships are complex because people are complex. Neither can ever be reduced to a single theory, be expressed in a single approach to life, or be contained in a single self-help book.

Chart 15.1—Behavioral Characteristics

Common Personal Characteristics:

Abrupt	Determined	Responsible
Aggressive	Decisive	Self-Reliant
Bold	Domineering	Strong-Minded
Competitive	Productive	Tough
Courageous	Restless	Unemotional

Preferred Work Tasks:

Buying	Enforcing	Planning
Debating	Judging	Problem solving
Deciding	Managing	Supervising
Delegating	Negotiating	Visualizing

Preferred Working Conditions:
Wants to have impact by creating new environments
Likes to exercise power and authority
Prefers large and challenging projects
Wants freedom from external controls
Wants opportunities for financial success

Responds Best To:
An impersonal approach
Direct, honest confrontation
Fair, open competition
Getting results quickly
Logical, rational arguments

Chart 15.2—Cognitive Characteristics

Common Personal Characteristics:

Accurate	Indecisive	Strict
Analytical	Loyal	Structured
Cautious	Organized	Theoretical
Conscientious	Perceptive	Unsociable
Critical	Perfectionistic	Worrisome

Preferred Work Tasks:

Analyzing	Classifying	Proofreading
Appraising	Computing	Recording
Calculating	Editing	Reviewing
Clarifying	Measuring	Tabulating

Preferred Working Conditions:
Seeks quiet, organized working spaces
Wants to work with competent co-workers or alone
Prefers to work on specialized, task-oriented projects
Expects to have an impact on the quality of products
Likes positions with limited responsibilities over others
Needs structured activities and clear directions

Responds Best To:
Diplomatic, factual challenges
Arguments based on known facts
Freedom from competitive strain
Tasks which are clear and easy to accomplish
Non-aggressive behaviors

Chart 15.3—Interpersonal Characteristics

Common Personal Characteristics:

Careful	Hardworking	Slow
Calm	Lenient	Stubborn
Dependent	Likeable	Understanding
Faithful	Unassertive	Warm

Preferred Work Tasks:

Arranging	Mediating	Reflecting
Assisting	Ordering	Relating
Balancing	Organizing	Supporting
Filing	Processing	Typing

Preferred Working Conditions:
Prefers surroundings which are harmonious
Seeks team-member and support-role positions
Works toward practical and useful results
Likes organized living and working environments
Wants to work with others to improve things
Needs guaranteed security

Responds Best To:
A gradual approach to challenging
Practical approaches to problem solving
Comfortable, friendly conversations
Conventional, well-proven methods
Honest and clear communications

Chart 15.4—Affective Characteristics

Common Personal Characteristics:

Appealing	Flexible	Open-Minded
Compassionate	Friendly	Restless
Convincing	Impulsive	Talkative
Creative	Intuitive	Undisciplined
Enthusiastic	Loud	Unproductive

Preferred Work Tasks:

Coaching	Entertaining	Selling
Counseling	Performing	Training
Creating	Promoting	Traveling
Demonstrating	Public Speaking	Writing

Preferred Working Conditions:

Wants to have impact on people by selling ideas
Seeks positions of mobility and recognition
Dislikes having to account for details
Likes opportunities for creative expression
Prefers unstructured activities and routines
Works best with a boss who has a democratic style

Responds Best To:

Being challenged in an exciting way
An influencing, creative sales pitch
Affection and personal attention
Having a good time
Group activities

PART FIVE

THE DEEPER SEARCH
FOR PERSONAL STYLE

Chapter 16.
Keep Thinking About That Puzzle Piece

For you created my inmost being; you knit me together in my mother's womb. I praise you because I am fearfully and wonderfully made.

— King David
Psalm 139:13-14

Finding the Source

What is the source of personal style? Where do the four dimensions come from? How are they created within us? Are they part of our genetic inheritance? Why does Bill prefer a direct approach to whatever he encounters in the environment around him? Why does Connie like to react with caution instead? What makes Isabella perceive the environment as big and overwhelming? Why is Andy so adventurous and playful?

No one really knows exactly—at least not yet—because it is difficult to isolate the causes of these dimensions of our behavior. We also do not know why there are only four dimensions instead of three or seven. However, from the scientific research on physiological functioning of the brain, we can make some good hunches about where differences in personal style may physiologically originate. Although at this point in time no single theory has been formulated to offer a complete explanation of the brain, a fascinating picture is beginning to emerge.

Is It the Reticular Activating System?

It is impossible for us to be active without a normally functioning nervous system, because this is the main communication network from the brain to the other parts of the body. We actually have two nervous systems. Each one plays a vital role in keeping us interacting effectively with the environment we live in.

One system is the *peripheral nervous system,* which consists of all the body's nerves that are *not* located within the brain and spinal cord. This nervous system is responsible for transmitting information from the body to the central nervous system (i.e., muscles, glands, sensory organs) and back again.

The second main subdivision of the nervous system is the *central nervous system.* It contains all the nerve networks within the brain and spinal cord. The brain functions as a command center, while the spinal cord acts as a super highway from the brain to the rest of the body. Every day electrochemical messages sent from the brain stimulate millions of bodily functions, and in turn, the brain receives millions of messages back from the body using this superhighway. Along this highway is a special section of roadway called the *reticular activating system (RAS).*

The RAS is an assembly of individual sensory neurons (nerve cells) within the brain stem. It is essential to the central nervous system because it controls how people are aroused by, pay attention to, and concentrate on, what is occurring within the environment. In 1989, Dr. David Myers, professor of psychology at Hope College, described the role of the RAS this way:

> Inside the brain stem, extending from the spinal cord right up into the thalamus, is a finger-sized network of neurons called the reticular activating system (also called the reticular formation). Most of the spinal cord axons of sensory neurons travel up to the thalamus. Along the way, some of them branch off to the adjacent reticular system. Thus, when sensory stimulation occurs, the reticular system is activated. The reticular system transmits information about its state to the cerebral cortex, which in turn arouses the brain. . . . Under the influence of the cortex, the reticular system controls not only arousal but also attention (p. 36).

It seems likely that the source of personal style differences can be attributed to the RAS. The degree of reticular activation development in a person will determine how that person reacts to, and is motivated by, environmental stimuli. Certain stimuli will arouse; other stimuli will have little effect. In short, a person's level of sensitivity to the environment is directly related to RAS development.

Because the degree of this development varies from person to person, environmental factors that stimulate one person to act in a certain manner may not stimulate another person to behave in the same way. The different styles of behavior we note in ourselves and others could therefore be closely connected to how "environmentally sensitive" RAS development has made us. That RAS has influence on our basic personal tendencies is maintained by W.P. Blitchington (1983), who states the following:

> In fact, whether you're an introvert or an extrovert depends largely upon your RAS. There are other contributions to be sure. But people who inherit an "overdeveloped" RAS will be predisposed toward introversion. Those who inherit an "underdeveloped" RAS will more likely become extroverts (p. 14).

The effect of RAS on personal style becomes clearer if we focus on a specific area of behavior. As introversion and extroversion figure prominently into personal style— composing one of the personal style continuums (see Chapter 7)—and lend themselves well to the subject of RAS, let's pursue them further.

What About Introversion/Extroversion?

Whatever the environment, all individuals try to behave in such ways that increase their levels of comfort and decrease their levels of discomfort. This reaction, or sensitivity, to environmental stimuli can be discussed within the framework of extroversion and introversion. Extroversion signifies a person's tendency to focus outside the self; introversion denotes a person's tendency to focus inward toward the self. Most people are a blend of extroversion and introversion, yet each of us tends to favor one mode of behavior over the other, depending on the situation.

Extroverts need relatively strong levels of stimuli to become aroused. Introverts tend to be more reactive to environmental stimuli than extroverts because they are more sensitive to weaker stimuli than extroverts; that is, they are more easily aroused by weak stimuli. The link between extroversion/ introversion and arousal levels is theoretical; however, as Hans and Michael Eysenck, two British psychologists who have pioneered research into the relationship between brain function and extroversion/introversion, pointed out:

> Many such studies (of electroencephalographic brain waves, now measurable with such accuracy, of heart rate, of the electric conductivity of the skin, of breathing rate, of changes in pupil diameter, etc.) have now been carried out, and in general support the theory that extroversion/introversion is linked to levels of arousal. . . . Extroverts, as we have seen, have a low level of arousal, whereas introverts have a high level. In fact, most people seek intermediate levels of arousal. Too high or too low a level of arousal is unpleasant, and people will try to avoid them (pp. 172-173).

It should be noted that this avoidance of "unpleasant" levels of arousal supports the contention that indeed there is connection between RAS development and behavior patterns (personal styles).

We can see how this link between arousal and extroversion/introversion may be at work in the four personal style dimensions. Individuals like Isabella and Connie, who have strong tendencies toward introversion, are apt be quite sensitive to environmental stimuli such as loud noises, crowded rooms, and aggressive strangers; they will retreat from or avoid powerful stimuli like these, which strain their nervous systems. Individuals like Andy and Bill, who are prone to extroversion, will be less sensitive to environmental stimuli. They will be drawn by or seek out strong stimuli in order to maintain active levels of interest in the environment.

Because the RAS also influences individual attention levels, it makes sense that individuals like Connie and Isabella tend to pay close attention to weaker stimuli and withdraw from or avoid stronger ones. Their sensitivity often makes them so attentive to environmental stimuli that they feel overwhelmed by what is happening around them. At this point their stress levels rise, necessitating escape to the kind of environment they prefer, one in which they feel secure or can predict what is going to happen next. This overattentiveness is linked to their tendency to magnify, distort, or in other ways generally overreact to experiences that are stressful or exert pressure on them.

Bill and Andy, on the other hand, being less sensitive to what is happening around them, are usually uninterested in weak stimuli. They prefer action and pay closer attention to more intense stimuli, which can motivate them and incite them to become more active. They will take risks in order to become aroused by environmental stimuli and have a tendency to underreact to situations in which there is not enough pressure; thus they prefer large groups and lively situations, whereas introverts like Connie and Isabella would prefer small groups and quiet surroundings.

Although the two pairs—Connie and Isabella, Bill and Andy—share their respective bonds of introversion and extroversion, these individuals are also quite distinct from their partners in regards to the people-oriented/task-oriented continuum. Connie and Bill are more task-oriented, whereas Isabella and Andy tend to be people-oriented. As the RAS seems to influence the extroversion/introversion continuum, is there perhaps a biophysical reason why individuals will fall at one end of this continuum rather than the other? Some people think so, and they attribute our tendencies in this continuum to whether we are predominantly "right-brain" or "left-brain" thinkers.

Don't Forget to Think Right and Left

The human brain has two main divisions: the left hemisphere and the right hemisphere. Each hemisphere gathers information and "learns" separately from the other, processing and storing information in its own unique manner. Each one has specific responsibilities in the process of thinking and sending messages to the body. For example, the left side ("left brain") is language-oriented and in charge of specialized thinking (logical, sequential, and analytical modes). The right side ("right brain") is more perceptual and emotional, focusing on total integration of knowledge (intuitive, holistic, and symbolic modes). The left side controls fine muscle behaviors (such as writing or typing), while the right side controls large muscle movements (like playing football or dancing).

These two "halves" or sides of the brain are connected by the corpus callosum (a large band of neural fibers), that functions like a communication bridge, allowing information to move back and forth between the two sides. In studies on individuals where the corpus callosum had been severed due to injury, mental commands still passed through the brain stem to both sides of the body even though information sharing between the left and right halves of the brain had stopped. This seems to indicate that each side of the brain can function to some degree without the other side.

It appears that one reason why the four personal style dimensions are different from one another is that human brains *process information* in different ways. Studies on split-brain thinking suggest that individuals possess cognitive differences in thinking due to left-right brain preferences, therefore, it is possible that each personal style dimension is controlled by either the left or right side of the brain, which in turn would influence perceptions and behavior accordingly. In fact, people with behavioral and cognitive styles appear to display more left-brain tendencies, while people with interpersonal and affective styles exhibit more right-brain tendencies. How the brain tends to process information may determine how strong each of the four dimensions are. Personal style dimensions, therefore, may be strongly developed by split-brain thinking that is preset before birth.

In 1984, Donovan and Wonder published *Whole-Brain Thinking,* in which they extensively discuss the main functions of both sides of the brain. Their book is intriguing to read. In particular, the following points from their book support personal style theory:

1. The human brain's two halves have different but overlapping skills and ways of thinking.

2. Individuals have a tendency to prefer one side or the other, which affects their approach to life and work. Although individuals do not change dominance or preference, it is possible to develop the skills of the less-preferred hemisphere.

3. Thatever your dominance or preference, you still use both sides of your brain and shift between them, depending upon the skills needed and the particular way that your brain handles information.

4. Lateralization is the degree to which brain functions are performed in the task-appropriate hemisphere (balancing the checkbook in the left and recalling a loved one's face in the right). Highly lateralized individuals move more completely into the task-appropriate hemisphere (the usual case with males), while less lateralized persons will perform a task in both hemisphere (the usual case with females).

Chart 16.1 summarizes all of these personal style differences as they relate to RAS development and left-right brain preferences. The chart represents the state of our current knowledge about the origins of personal style preferences. It is an incomplete picture and will need to be revised in the future as additional findings are revealed.

Chart 16.1—Factors Influencing Personal Style Development			
	BEHAVIORAL	**COGNITIVE**	**INTERPERSONAL**	**AFFECTIVE**

	BEHAVIORAL	COGNITIVE	INTERPERSONAL	AFFECTIVE
BRAIN SIDE PREFERENCE	Left	Left	Right	Right
RAS DEVELOPMENT	Less Developed	More Developed	More Developed	Less Developed
AROUSAL LEVEL	Less Sensitive to the Environment	More Sensitive to the Environment	More Sensitive to the Environment	Less Sensitive to the Environment
ATTENTION LEVEL	Motivated by Strong Stimuli	Motivated by Minor Stimuli	Motivated by Minor Stimuli	Motivated by Strong Stimuli
ENVIRONMENTAL APPROACH	Extroverted	Introverted	Introverted	Extroverted

Putting RAS and Left-Right Thinking Together

It is possible that the influence of both RAS development and left-right brain preferences accounts for a wide range of personal style similarities and differences. By themselves, these processes do not seem to provide a complete explanation for how personal style is developed, but the two together perhaps provide us with the best evidence to date that they are instrumental in personal style development. If indeed these processes work in conjunction, then each personal style dimension could be determined by the interaction (or blending) of brain-side preference and RAS functioning. Interestingly enough, this might help to explain why individuals are similar in certain characteristics while different in others. Obviously, there may also be other factors involved.

Let's assume there is a blending effect occurring between these two phenomena. Uncovering its existence would help us to better understand the development of personal style differences. Then, the information known about brain-side functioning and extroversion/introversion could be matched with the characteristics for each of the personal style dimensions. The relationships identified in Chart 16.2 could then be suggested as a possible answer to our question of physiological origin.

Chart 16.2—The Influence of Biological Factors on Style

Left Brain/Extroversion	=	The Behavioral Dimension
Left Brain/Introversion	=	The Cognitive Dimension
Right Brain/Introversion	=	The Interpersonal Dimension
Right Brain/Extroversion	=	The Affective Dimension

Pursuing this idea further, let's see if it fits what is already known about our four characters. First of all, Bill is indeed an extrovert who prefers left-brain thinking. Connie is also left-brain dominant, but is introverted rather than extroverted like Bill. While Isabella is introverted like Connie, she is right brain dominant like Andy. Andy is extroverted like Bill, yet right-brain thinking like Isabella. This is just as we would expect, and it suggests that the following relationships between the two phenomena cause the personal style differences that are identified as personal style dimensions.

Chart 16.3—Biological Factors and Personal Style Dimensions

	Introversion	Extroversion
Left Brain	Connie	Bill
Right Brain	Isabella	Andy

It seems that once you understand the organizing principle involved, you see many things in everyday life that fit the four-quadrant model.

— **Ned Herrmann**

Information Processing: Two Sections or Four?

Recent research suggests that a quad-brain approach is more useful for identifying thinking processes than the split-brain approach. A pioneer in this method for understanding how brain function influences personality and behavior is Ned Herrmann. His findings, presented in his 1990 book, *The Creative Brain*, strongly support personal style theory.

Hermann describes his four-quadrant theory of brain functioning as follows:

> The limbic system was also divided into two separated halves, and also endowed with a cortex capable of thinking, and also connected by a commissure—just like the cerebral hemispheres. Instead of there being two parts of the specialized brain, there were four—the number of clusters the data had been showing! . . . So, what I had been calling left brain, would now become the left cerebral hemisphere. What was the right brain, now became the right cerebral hemisphere. What had been left center, would now be left limbic, and right center, now right limbic (p. 63).

The Creative Brain is one of the most extensive investigations of brain functioning I have encountered, and I highly recommend it to anyone interested in a more complete review of this subject. It also comes closest to examining what personal style theory explores: the possibility that people have distinct thinking processes that influence, and maybe even create, their preferences for certain styles of behavior. Both the four-quadrant theory and personal style theory seek to understand the mysteries of human behavior; in a sense, they both ask, "Why aren't you more like me?" In our search for the answer to this question, we continue a tradition that runs throughout human history, for there have been other theories of human behavior, other explorers, many of whom have focused in their own ways on personal style.

References

If you would like to explore further how others have discussed the relationship between style and personality, you will find it useful to start with the references below.

Blitchington, W. P. (1983). *The energy and vitality book*. Wheaton, Illinois: Tyndale House Publishers, Inc.

Donovan, P., & Wonder, J. (1984). *Whole brain thinking*. New York, New York: William Morrow and Company.

Eysenck, H. J., & Eysenck, M. (1983). *Mindwatching: Why people behave the way they do*. Garden City, New Jersey: Anchor Press, Doubleday.

Herrman, N. (1990). *The creative brain*. Lake Lure, North Carolina: Brain Books.

Myers, D. (1989). *Psychology*. (1st and 2nd eds.). New York, New York: Worth.

Chapter 17.
The Name Game

We shall not cease from exploration
And the end of all our exploring
Will be to arrive where we started
And to know the place for the first time.

— T.S. Eliot

Earlier Explorations

There is nothing new about personal style. Its influence on people's behavior has been recognized throughout history. Although known by a variety of different names, the same basic phenomenon has been described many times before. This is comforting. It suggests that even though our understanding of the origin of personal style is far from complete, we are dealing with something quite fundamental in the make-up of human beings.

Underlying all of the many differences and idiosyncrasies in our personalities, there seem to be four basic types of preferred behavior. These same four dimensions of personal style have been identified and studied repeatedly by different theorists, who have used terminology such as *personality types*, *psychological types*, *communication styles*, *social styles*, and *temperament* to explain what we call personal style dimensions. Let's take a quick look at some of the better-known theorists and their style systems.

It All Started With Greek "Humour"

The earliest-known personal style investigation was conducted by the Greek physician Hippocrates, the "father of medicine," who lived in the second half of the fifth century B.C. He believed that human behavior was controlled by natural forces and that the four elements—earth, water, air, and fire—were directly connected to the personality. His theory posited that each element had a different effect on human physiology, particularly on four types of vital fluids—black bile, phlegm, blood, and yellow bile—which he called *humours*.

From personal style theory's point of view, the four humours would correspond to the four personal style dimensions. These humours, which according to Hippocrates were produced by the liver, supposedly had a direct influence on an individual's personality and behavior. When each humour left the liver and entered the bloodstream, it would change the personality in some predictable way. Chart 17.1 illustrates the links between the major factors in Hippocrates' theory and their ultimate effects on the personality (chart developed by Anderson; see Anderson & Robinson, 1988, p. 20).

Chart 17.1 — Hippocrates' Model

Element	Qualities	Humour	Effect
Earth	cold, dry	melancholy (black bile)	sadness
Water	cold, moist	phlegm	quietness
Air	hot, moist	blood	aggressiveness
Fire	hot, dry	choler (yellow bile)	restlessness

Hippocrates' theory led the Greeks to believe that these different fluids shaped body and head size in a specific way, and that a person's physique was therefore a personality indicator. For example, individuals who were muscular in build supposedly had personalities that differed from those people who were skinny or heavy, and people with larger heads were of a different personality type than people with smaller heads. Although this "reading of" physical differences didn't survive the passing of time, Hippocrates' theory and classification of personality differences did.

Hippocrates' theory was further popularized by Galen, another famous Greek physician. Using Hippocrates' theory he called the four dimensions of behavior *sanguine* (happy), *choleric* (restless), *melancholic* (sad) and *phlegmatic* (reserved). He included in his theory the concept that varying levels of health were associated with each one of the different personality types. Galen's theory and classifications lasted well into the Renaissance. His terminology lasted even longer. Just prior to the turn of the twentieth century, one of the founding fathers of the study of psychology, Wilhelm Wundt, used these same four terms to describe and categorize personality characteristics. While he dropped many of the physiological associations with these four dimensions, he realized there was some "truth" to these classifications of personality.

These same Greek terms were not popularized again until Tim and Bev LaHaye (1966), who wrote several best sellers on style differences, rediscovered them in the Sixties. In 1983, Florence Littauer, who was inspired by the LaHayes, adopted the four phases and began to use them in all of her publications. In her latest book (1992) she has renamed the four original terms with the labels "Powerful Choleric," "Perfect Melancholic," "Peaceful Phlegmatic," and "Popular Sanguine."

After the Bile Trial Came the Swiss Twist

Many writers and theorists have developed a variety of similar models and terms to explain personality style differences. Perhaps the best known of these approaches was constructed by the Swiss psychiatrist Carl Jung, who founded analytical psychology. His model included two newly identified characteristics: *introversion* and *extroversion*, and was structured on four personality characteristics: *sensing, feeling, thinking, and intuitive*. Jungian psychology has provided the theoretical background upon which many other people have produced inventories and questionnaires of personality characteristics. Perhaps the most well known of these inventories is the Myers-Briggs Type Indicator (MBTI). It has been used extensively for many years in studies examining personal style differences. (See Myers & McCaulley, 1985, for further information on the MBTI).

Other well-known psychologists and theorists also developed variations on Jungian theory. One theorist in particular, Marston (1927), attempted to use a list of personality characteristics to help individuals identify which style dimension best fit their personality. This word list from Marston's work was adopted by Geier (1977) and became the basis for the Personal Profile System (PPS). Many other groups have adopted Marston and Geier's work into their own assessments, using with minor changes Marston's original word list. These systems are often referred to as the DISC (Dominance, Influence, Steadiness, and Compliance) systems. Paltiel (1986) and Johnson, Wood, and Blinkhorn (1988) offer reviews of these types of systems.

Other psychologists who build models that contributed to style aware-ness would include Lewin (1936), Horney (1942), and Fromm (1964). All three added some new "twists" to the style discussion while still using a four-dimensional approach to identify and classify personality types. Lewin focused on how individuals perceive and interact with the envi-ronment. Horney's model introduced the concept of understanding per-sonal style differences by examining differences in interpersonal inter-actions. And Fromm's approach introduced concepts that centered on how people manipulate or submit to others. Merrill and Reid (1981) con-tinued in this direction of classification with their development of social styles.

A most interesting description of the four personal style dimensions was presented by Gary Smalley and John Trent (1990) in their book *The Two Sides of Love.* Using right-brain creativity to formulate "word pictures," they identified the four dimensions as animal characters— Lion, Otter, Beaver, and Golden Retriever. And there are several other popular theories on personal style differences that are worth looking at, although they do not use four-dimensional models.

For instance, John Holland's Personality Types (Realistic, Investi-gative, Artistic, Conventional, Social, and Enterprising) form one well-known style model that uses six styles in its classification system (Hol-land, 1973). These personality types have been used extensively in occu-pational surveys such as the Strong-Campbell Interest Inventory and Holland's Self-Directed Search. They are also used in books such as the *Dictionary of Holland Occupational Codes*; (Gottfredson & Holland, 1989) to list and organize careers into different classifications. These types of career-search aids allow individuals to access job information using their personality types.

Models such as the Myers-Briggs Type Indicator and Holland's Per-sonality Types are not easily matched with personal style theory. It is difficult to suggest comparisons between these theories because there are structural differences in the models. For example, the MBTI ap-proach differs from personal style theory most notably in its design. The PSI model is build upon a three-continuum axis (Extroversion/Introver-sion, Nonverbal/Verbal, and Task-Oriented/People-Oriented) while the MBTI is derived from a four-continuum model (Extroversion/Introver-sion, Sensing/Intuition, Thinking/Feeling, and Judging/Perceiving). Even so, it is still quite evident that both models are describing the same sets of personality characteristics and simply using a different number of classifications.

Making comparisons between these two models and the Personal Style Model is difficult—and risky—because the structures of the models are different: nevertheless, due to the popularity of these two models, many people have asked me to include some information on how they might interface with the PSI dimensions, and I have tried to respond to this request in a helpful way. As well as possible, I have matched the six dimensions from each of these two models with the four dimensions used by the Personal Style Model. In doing so, I have identified three characteristics from each of the other two models that can be correlated with each of the dimensions used in the Personal Style Model. The result is Chart 17.2. I hope you will find it a useful comparison.

Chart 17.2 — Comparing the PSI with Holland's Classifications and the MBTI

PSI	Holland's Codes	MBTI
Behavioral	Realistic, Enterprising, Investigative	Extroversion, Sensing, Thinking, Judging
Cognitive	Conventional, Investigative, Realistic	Introversion, Sensing, Thinking, Judging
Interpersonal	Social, Conventional, Artistic	Introversion, Intuition, Feeling, Perceiving
Affective	Enterprising, Artistic, Social	Extroversion, Intuition, Feeling, Perceiving

It is fascinating to investigate the similarities between these previous approaches to the study of personal style. As we have seen, there are many other significant approaches too, and to encourage you to continue your investigation of the history of style, I've supplied Chart 17.3. Each one of the theorist's models identified in this chart categorizes personality differences using a four-dimensional approach. Each category has been listed under the personal style dimension that best fits its description. For your convenience, I have included the main works of these theorists in the references section at the end of the chapter (pp. 200-201).

Chart 17.3 — Previous Names for Personal Style Dimensions

THEORIST	BEHAVIORAL	COGNITIVE	INTERPERSONAL	AFFECTIVE
Hippocrates/Galen 5th Century B.C.	Choleric	Melancholic	Phlegmatic	Sanguine
Marston, W., 1927	Dominance	Compliance	Submission	Inducement
Jung, C., 1928	Sensing	Thinking	Feeling	Intuitive
Lewin, K., 1936	Concrete Experiences	Abstract Conceptualization	Reflective Observation	Active Experimentation
Horney, K., 1942	Moving Toward People— Aggressive Type	Moving Away From People— Detached Type	Moving Toward People— Compliant Type	Moving Toward People— Proving-Self Type
Fromm, E., 1964	Exploitive/ Manipulative Orientation	Hoarding Orientation	Receptive/ Dependent Orientation	Marketing Orientation
LaHaye, T., 1966	Choleric	Melancholic	Phlegmatic	Sanguine
Grier, J., 1977	Dominance	Compliance	Steadiness	Influencing
Herrman, N., 1978	Lower Left/ Limbic	Upper Left/ Cerebral	Lower Right/ Limbic	Upper Right/ Cerebral
Merrill, D. & Reid, R., 1981	Driving	Analytical	Amiable	Expressive
Smalley, G.& Trent, J., 1990	Lion	Beaver	Golden Retriever	Otter
Littauer, F., 1992	Powerful Choleric	Perfect Melancholic	Peaceful Phlegmatic	Popular Sanguine

References

Anderson, T. D., & Robinson, E. (1988). *The leader's manual for the Personal Style Indicator and the Job Style Indicator*. Abbotsford, BC: Consulting Resource Group International, Inc.

Fromm, E. (1964). *The heart of man*. New York, New York: Harper and Row.

Galen (1981). *On the doctrines of Hippocrates and Plato*. (2nd ed.; P. DeLacy, Trans.) Berlin, Germany: Akademie-Verlag.

Geier, J. (1977). *The personal profile system*. Performax Systems International, Inc.

Gottfredson, G. D. & Holland, J. L. (1989). *Dictionary of Holland Occupational Codes*. Odessa, Florida: Psychological Assessment Resources, Inc.

Holland, J. L. (1973). *Making vocational choices: A theory of careers.* Englewood Cliffs, New Jersey: Prentice-Hall.

Horney, K. (1942). *Self-analysis.* New York, New York: Norton.

Johnson, C., Wood, R., & Blinkhorn, S. (1988). Spuriouser and spuriouser: The use of ipsative personality tests. *Journal of Occupational Psychology, 61*(2), 153-162.

Jung, C. (1923). *Psychological types.* London, England: Routledge.

Jung, C. (1928). *Contributions to Analytic Psychology.* New York, New York: New American Library.

LaHaye, T. (1966). *Spirit-controlled temperament.* Illinois: Tyndale House.

Lewin, K. (1936). *Principles of topological and vectoral psychology.* New York, New York: McGraw Hill.

Littauer, F. (1983). *Personality plus.* Michigan: Fleming H. Revell.

Littauer, F., & Littauer, M. (1992). *Personality puzzle.* Michigan: Fleming H. Revell.

Marston, W. (1927, July-Sept.). Motor consciousness as a basis for emotion. *Journal of Abnormal and Social Psychology, XXII*, 140-150.

Merrill, D. & Reid, R. (1981). *Personal styles and effective performance.* Radnor, Pennsylvania: Chilton Book Company.

Myers, I., & McCaulley, H. (1985). *Manual: A guide to the development and use of the Myers-Briggs Type Indicator.* Palo Alto, California: Consulting Psychologists Press.

Paltiel, L. (1986). Self-appraisal personality inventories. *Guidance and Assessment Review, 2*(3), 3-7.

Smalley, G., & Trent, J. (1990). *The two sides of love.* Pomona, California: Focus on the Family.

Wundt, W. (1904). *Principles of physiological psychology.* (Vol. 1; E.B. Tichener, Trans.). London: Swan, Sonnenschein

Chapter 18.
One Piece Isn't the Whole Puzzle

Don't mistake pleasure for happiness.
They are a different breed of dog.

— Josh Billings

The Essentials for Happiness

After 30 years Dave and I are still best friends. Just the other day he was trying to teach me how to golf. "Goof" would have been a better name for what I was actually doing. Sooner or later I am confident that I will graduate from the driving range. Years of miniature golf have left some bad habits, but Dave promised that once I can hit the ball over 50 feet, we'll slide onto the fairway. He's still making things look easy while I'm still struggling to keep up. After all we both have been through in life, our styles haven't changed all that much. What is important is that we are both happy being who we are. Happiness doesn't always come from playing games and taking part in pleasurable events, and it comes from different things within each one of us.

As was explained at the beginning of this book, personal style is only one part of your personality. Although it is a very important part, you should not focus on it at the expense of the other personality development factors mentioned in Chapter 5, such as your self-worth level and the social teachers you have known. Understanding these other pieces to the human puzzle are also essential for healthy living and happiness. In an odd sort of way, happiness is simply learning to be content with what you have and where you are in any given moment, even when what you have and where you are do not provide you with much pleasure.

The Journey Home

As I have mentioned, for so long I searched to find some way of explaining why other people I came across tended to be so different from me. They appeared similar enough to me on the surface, but underneath they seemed to think and behave totally opposite from me. I couldn't understand how they could perceive their environment so differently. They picked up signals I couldn't read, they put importance on matters I ignored, and they became angry at things I thought were trivial—I'm sure they thought the same way about me too!

There were people like Bill who were doers. They were productive and energetic. They always seemed to be focusing on results and how to get them. They were bold, direct, and authoritative. Then there were individuals like Connie who were analysts, checking through any available information. They identified problems, perceived trends, and offered solutions. They were so careful, sensitive, and critical. In contrast, there were others like Andy who were sellers. They were persuasive and influential. They always seemed have people around them, watching what they were doing or listening to what they had to say. They were creative, intuitive and self-assured. Finally, there were people like Isabella who were easygoing and whose feet were firmly planted on the ground. They were consistent team players, always encouraging others and helping them out. This sort of person was friendly, accepting, and dependable.

As I read more widely, I learned that these four basic types of behavior had been recognized down through the ages by a variety of writers and thinkers. Slowly, a clearer picture emerged for me. It revealed how people were different and why they seemed to be hearing different voices and marching to a different drummer. I began to understand what personal differences were all about and how styles of preferred interaction with the environment lay beneath much of the unexplained behavior I witnessed in people. The concept of personal style was exhilarating and powerful. It offered an intriguingly simple model that enveloped so much of what before had been dizzying confusion. It led me out of the forest and returned me home to who I really was. It lifted the blinders from my eyes and opened a new window onto the world. It provided me with a new view of life, a view that truly helped me to be happier.

Key Concepts Clarify the View

To help bring the picture of the puzzle into proper focus, let's review some of the main ideas about personal style theory that were presented in previous chapters of this book.

1. Personal style is only part of one's personality.

While personal style greatly influences what you think, say, and do, it doesn't constitute your complete personality. Your personality consists of more than just your personal style.

2. Personal style is only one developmental factor.

Personal style is only one out of six categories of factors that influence the development of your personality. The other five categories are:

1. Biophysical Influences
2. Social Teachers
3. Traumatic Experiences
4. Environmental Systems
5. Self-Worth Levels

Individuals with the same style patterns will behave differently because they will be influenced by other factors of personality development. For example, personal style does not determine individual levels of ability, intelligence, or morality. These characteristics are determined by factors that come from categories other than personal style.

3. Personal style is essentially fixed.

Every person appears to have a particular style that is preset from birth. Personal style does not change much over time. It is that part of your personality that remains constant during the aging process, regardless of life experiences. While the source of personal styles is not certain, a strong possibility could be the interaction of the following:

- RAS Development/Extroversion-Introversion
- Right-Brain/Left-Brain Processes and Preferences

Whatever your personal style, it is unlikely to alter much throughout your lifetime; therefore, learning how to understand it and work with it to achieve greater personal development is more advantageous than trying to alter it to another personal style. This does not mean you cannot change things in your life. You can certainly improve how you get along with others and how effective you are in different situations, but although you can develop your style, you can't swap it for another one.

4. Everyone has a personal style pattern.

Personal style consists of the influences of four personal style dimensions. The combination of the four style dimensions creates a pattern that is stronger than any one dimension alone. The interactions between these dimensions create a style of behavior that is essentially unique, but the style is likely to correspond closely to one of 21 possible personal style patterns. These (21 patterns are profiled *The PSI In-Depth Interpretations Booklet* . See note page 53.) No personal style pattern is better than any other; each pattern is appropriate in certain situations.

5. Personal style patterns have four different dimensions.

Every individual's personal style pattern consists of four style dimensions: behavioral, cognitive, interpersonal and affective. These dimensions have been known for quite some time, down through the centuries. No dimension is better than another. Each dimension is unique in how it influences personality and behavior. The weaker dimensions are just as important to understand as the stronger dimensions.

6. Personal style patterns determine style flexibility.

The *Personal Style Indicator* (PSI) helps you to reveal the strength of these dimensions in your particular style. Dimensions with scores above 40 dominate the pattern more than dimensions with scores below 40. Due to the different combinations of dimensions that are possible, some individuals have higher levels of style flexibility than others. Style-flexibility can be learned by anyone who wishes to develop their style shifting skills.

7. Personal style influences environmental interactions.

The dimensions of personal style affect how we naturally prefer to deal with our surroundings. These dimensions strongly influence each individual's ability to perceive, approach, and interact with the environment. Different perceptions lead to different mental and behavioral strengths and limitations. Different approaches to the environment lead to different individual styles of interactions. Different interactions with others in the environment then lead to different levels of success in various social settings.

8. Personal style influences energy levels.

Every individual has a varying level of intensity in each personal style dimension. Each dimension strongly affects physical (behavioral), mental (cognitive), emotional (interpersonal), and creative (affective) energies within the body. People tend to overdevelop skill areas that are related to their strongest energy levels, and to avoid developing skill areas that are associated with weaker energy levels. For example, a person who is strong in the behavioral dimension will tend to develop skill areas that involve physical energy, whereas another person may avoid developing mental skill areas because he or she is weak in the cognitive dimension.

9. Personal style underlies other styles.

All other styles of interactive behavior are influenced by personal style, such as teaching styles, management styles, leadership styles, and parenting styles. Personal style also appears to act as the foundation for our interpersonal styles (e.g., passive, aggressive). Our interpersonal styles are a combination of our personal style and of the social attitudes and behaviors we have learned.

Certain personal style dimensions influence individuals to be more passive, while other ones lead people toward being more aggressive. Regardless of a person's personal style, anyone can learn how to be in charge of their behavior and be more successful in various social settings. Style-shifting is the best method I have found to successfully help individuals learn to be appropriately assertive.

10. Interpersonal skills can be developed.

It is better to accept and develop your style than to behave as if you were another style. Interpersonal skills can be developed to offset weaker dimensions and to develop flexibility. While natural preferences may not change, you can learn how to behave in ways that are not as natural for you. For instance, having a low score in the affective dimension would indicate that you are not very keen on performing before large crowds, but through training and experience you may learn to overcome this personal preference and become an expert performer.

11. Personal style does not determine who you are.

Nothing about your life is the direct result of your personal style. Personal style neither causes anything to happen nor prevents something from occurring. Whether you are a successful, happy, and wealthy person or an unfortunate, miserable, and poor one has nothing to do with your personal style. Personal style does have an influence, but it's only one factor among many that affect your life. You are limited just as much by heredity, circumstances, personal effort and other people's free will—to name just a few of the other determining factors. Each one of us is responsible for choosing how we will behave and which abilities we will develop even if other things hinder our route.

12. Your personal style is not good or bad.
Having a particular personal style doesn't make you more or less valuable as a person. Your importance to society and your significance to your loved ones, relatives, co-workers, neighbors, and friends is determined by shared experiences and not by your needs and preferences alone. Your personal style may become an asset or a liability in any particular set of circumstances you find yourself in, but this does not mean that your personal style is any better or worse than anybody else's.

Good Medicine, but Not a Cure-All

Personal style theory is not some grand unified theory of human nature that tries to explain everything. The four dimensions are not boxes into which we can neatly categorize people. Differences in the reticular activation system do not cause anything to happen. Variations in people's needs, values, and fears do not prove anything will happen. Knowing about personal style will not guarantee your life will become easier or happier as a direct result. Personal style is not a remedy that can solve things: only you can do that. It is not a road map that can tell you where to go: only you can decide that. Finally it is not some guru that can tell you how to lead your life: only you can discover that. There is more to life than personal style because there is more to YOU than your personal style.

The value of knowing about personal style is quite simple yet potent. By coming to recognize you have certain natural tendencies, that determine how you prefer to deal with the world, you can stop fretting over things that cannot be changed and begin to channel your efforts into things that can be changed. You learn to accept other people for what they are: different human beings. You can come to appreciate, even enjoy, those differences because you are no longer absorbed in the fruitless task of trying to change people or mold them into your own image.

Why Aren't I More Like You?

Throughout this book, I have used them, perhaps a little unfairly, as stereotypes for each dimension. I am sincerely glad that Bill, Connie, Andy, and Isabella are different from one other. I'm also glad that you and I are not the same. Just think how boring it would be if everyone had the same personal style. A world made up completely of Bills or Isabellas or Connies or Andys would be extremely dull because there would be no variety. For instance, could you imagine a world where everyone was strong only in the affective dimension? The party would never stop—and the work would never get done! Or how about everyone being like Isabella? We would all be willing to take orders and to follow, but whom would we follow and take orders from? Having differences in our styles is what makes life interesting, even if it also makes life frustrating at times too. But, whether positive or negative, style differences certainly add spice to human interaction.

Of course, the four characters presented are really only cardboard cutouts created for illustration purposes. No one is a pure type. We all have a Bill, a Connie, an Isabella, and an Andy within us to some degree. Perhaps it is strange that we have so much in common yet are still so different. But it is the differences among human beings that makes life interesting. I am not more like you and you are not more like me because each one of us is unique, each one of us is wonderfully made. A major part of our distinctiveness is accounted for by personal style, but not all of it. This is the point I want to leave you with. Never lose sight of the fact that we are more complex than any theory thought up by a human being can ever explain, and that includes personal style theory.

If we want to develop better relationships with those around us, we can. But we must take the initiative first. We must accept our responsibility for initiating change. We must want to achieve change, and we must be prepared to undertake the journey of self-discovery that allows change to be achieved. If this book has done anything, I hope it has helped to point the direction forward. Personal style may not be everything, but, as we have seen, it is an important beginning along the route to self-understanding. It is certainly not the whole picture, but for many people, like me, personal style is the missing piece in the puzzle of human interaction. It helps us understand that, from birth, we have different preferences for thinking and behaving. These differences should be acknowledged, accepted, and applied, rather than explained away. Only then can we begin to succeed with them.

Challenge yourself to take the personality puzzle apart for yourself. Move the pieces around until you get them to fit in the correct places for you. Understand which behaviors work for you and other people and which ones are costing you and others more than what you can afford. Don't let self-centeredness keep you from what counts most in life.

The Passion for Self-Fulfillment

This yearning has been with us a long time. The Ancient Greeks, as well as earlier civilizations, bequeathed us several myths exploring the meaning of this inner desire to comprehend our individuality. One of these myths tells the story of an extremely handsome youth named Narcissus. At his birth, his mother asked a local fortuneteller if the baby would live to a ripe old age. She was told he would, but only "if he never knows himself." Unfortunately for Narcissus, he was fated to fall in love with someone else—himself. It happened this way.

One hot summer's day, he stumbled across a tranquil mountain pool. Eagerly stooping down to quench his thirst, he suddenly saw a face looking back up at him from the surface of the water. It was the most beautiful person he had ever seen, and he became enamored with him, caught in the spell of his gaze, unable to look away. Narcissus desperately tried to reach into the water to pull this person toward him, but the figure vanished as his hands broke the water, only to return again once the water was calm. Every attempt proved fruitless, and he sat distraught, captivated by his own reflection and unable to see through his own vanity.

There is something of the misfortune of Narcissus in each of us. It is easy to become trapped within our preconceptions of ourselves and to become indifferent to the voices of others when we cannot translate what they are saying into anything more than echoes of our own beliefs. Like Narcissus, we risk falling in love with our own view of the world.

Somehow we have to break out of the confines of our own viewpoint so that we can appreciate how others see things. To do this, we need first to recognize that other people may indeed be seeing the world very differently than we do. *Why Aren't You More Like Me?* is intended to serve as a springboard to help the Narcissus living in each of us to break the surface, to dive beyond the edge of the pool of self-centeredness, to gain a perspective from which we have a view of how others perceive the world.

Exploring who we are—and who others are—can be a complicated and confusing task. Narcissus found himself stuck at the edge, mesmerized by his own reflection. To improve our personal understanding, we need to be prepared to go further, to enter the water and swim in it. Yet, when diving into unknown pools, we often find ourselves in deep and dangerous water. The water can be murky and deceptively turbulent. Sharp rocks may lurk beneath the surface and whirlpools may suddenly pull us under. So, if we're to go swimming around in the waters of our own personalities, we need to be on the lookout for any misconceptions or self-deceptions waiting to ensnare us. Here is the bottom line:

Either you control your self or your self will control you.

Make the Right Choice

Exploring who we are is very valuable, and it's the right choice if we use the information we find to care about others. When we keep what we learn to ourselves and use it to increase our gain while others suffer, we are making the wrong choice.

All human beings are self-centered. We have to be because we are so needy. For example, if I have just eaten a big lunch I will probably be more willing to give my food to others than if I haven't eaten in three days. In the first instance, my needs have been satisfied; in the second, they are strongly influencing me to put myself first. But being self-centered is not wrong as long as we are aware of it and take control over ourselves. When the self controls us, we become selfish; it is then that we don't share our food with others, whether if we are hungry or not.

Selfishness is one of the biggest weeds in the garden of personality. It destroys relationships. It destroys credibility. Most importantly of all, it destroys hope—hope of ever learning how to love and to be loved. Denying that you are self-centered will not make it go away; it will only make your self-centeredness stronger.

Why Aren't You More Like Me? can increase your self-control and your skills for dealing with people, but only if you are willing to let that happen. You are responsible for your behavior and how it affects your relationships. Regardless of how the cards have been dealt in your life, you must still play the hand you hold. No one else can take responsibility for you. Are you willing to change if you have to? I truly hope so.

APPENDIX

PERSONAL STYLE INDICATOR SHORT FORM

Personal Style Indicator (Short Form)

Have You Done the PSI?

This book presents a guide to understanding the significance of personal style. To fully appreciate the information being presented, you need to know in advance what your personal style is. Listed below are three possibilities. Choose the one that fits your situation and proceed as indicated.

1. If you have already completed the PSI, please ignore the rest of this section and begin reading Chapter 1.

2. If you have received a copy of the PSI accompanying this book, please work your way through it, following the instructions provided in it, before reading Chapter 1.

3. If you have not completed a PSI and do not have one handy at the moment, the following section will give you the opportunity to gain a rough idea of what your personal style is. While the results will not be as comprehensive as those obtained from using the full-length PSI instrument, they will at least help you to personalize the information discussed later in this book.

Directions

There are 16 sets of four words in the rating scale. Each row contains one set of four words. You are to rate each set of words using the numbers 1, 2, 3, 4. In doing so, decide how accurately the words describe your typical behavior with most people in most situations. Give the word that describes you most accurately a 4. Then give a 3 to the next word that describes you the best. Give a 2 to the next most descriptive word, and finally a 1 to the word that least describes how you might act. Rank all of the rows of words in this way.

For example, this is how I might rate the following set of four words:

Artistic—3   Technical—4   Productive—2   Supportive—1

The rating indicates that I think I'm more technical than I am artistic, more artistic than productive, more productive than supportive, and less supportive than any of the other three characteristics.

If you give a word a score of 4, it doesn't necessarily mean you always behave that way; it simply means you are more likely to behave in that way than in a way to which you give a 3. Likewise, giving a word a score of 1 doesn't mean you never behave in that way—just that you are less likely to behave in that way.

Make sure you only use the numbers 1 through 4, and do not give any half marks. You can only use each number once per row. Do not leave any spaces blank—rate all of the words in all of the rows.

Short Version of the PSI Response Sheet

1. ☐Certain   ☐Critical Thinker ☐Likeable   ☐Entertaining
2. ☐Unorganized ☐Shy   ☐Inflexible   ☐Domineering
3. ☐Calculating   ☐Trustworthy   ☐Outgoing   ☐Bold
4. ☐Stubborn   ☐Perfectionistic ☐Unemotional ☐Impulsive
5. ☐Tolerant   ☐Versatile   ☐Determined ☐Precise
6. ☐Unsociable   ☐Unappreciated ☐Self-Centered☐Passive
7. ☐Generous   ☐Direct   ☐Perceptive   ☐Patient
8. ☐Forceful   ☐Restless   ☐Slow-paced ☐Worrisome

Scoring Your Responses

Now that you have finished your ratings tally your responses by using the following steps:

1. Transfer your ratings to the spaces below.

1. ☐ Certain B	☐ Critical Thinker C	☐ Likeable I	☐ Entertaining A
2. ☐ Unorganized A	☐ Shy I	☐ Inflexible C	☐ Domineering B
3. ☐ Calculating C	☐ Trustworthy I	☐ Outgoing A	☐ Bold B
4. ☐ Stubborn I	☐ Perfectionistic C	☐ Unemotional B	☐ Impulsive A
5. ☐ Tolerant I	☐ Versatile A	☐ Determined B	☐ Precise C
6. ☐ Unsociable C	☐ Unappreciated B	☐ Self-Centered A	☐ Passive I
7. ☐ Generous A	☐ Direct B	☐ Perceptive C	☐ Patient I
8. ☐ Forceful B	☐ Restless A	☐ Slow-paced I	☐ Worrisome C

2. Now add up your ratings for each group of words with the same letter (B, C, I, A) and place the totals in the appropriate spaces below:

Total Scores For B _____	Total Scores For C _____	Total Scores For I _____	Total Scores For A _____	Should Equal 80
			=	_____

3. Check to be sure that the sum of the four total scores equals 80. If it does not, go back over you scores to locate mistakes in your arithmetic. If you are off by one or two points one way or another (e.g., 78 or 81), don't worry about it now, you can find your mistakes later. If you are off by more than a couple of points either way, then you should figure out where your mistake is.

4. To obtain your final scores, multiply each letter score by 2 and place the totals in the spaces below. These four totals should add up to 160.

B x 2 = _____   C x 2 = _____
I x 2 = _____   A x 2 = _____

Interpreting Your Results

5. Now make a graph of your final scores by using the diagram below. Draw a separate line across the page for each of your scores. Use the scale at the bottom of the graph for guidance.

B				
C				
I				
A				
20	**30**	**40**	**50**	**60**

Personal style is composed of four dimensions of behavior. That is why you have four final scores. These scores identify certain preferences you have for behaving in ways that are characteristic of each dimension. The letters on the left-hand side indicate the names of the four dimensions:

B	=	Behavioral
C	=	Cognitive
I	=	Interpersonal
A	=	Affective

Your personal style is influenced by these dimensions to different extents. Your scores reveal how strongly you prefer to behave in ways that are characteristic of each dimension. The higher your score, the greater your tendency for preferring a particular dimension. The unique characteristics of each dimension can be summarized as follows:

Behavioral

This style dimension is characterized by a strong tendency to alter the environment in such a way that well-defined goals can be achieved. Therefore, people who naturally operate mainly from this quadrant of style are likely to seem self-assured and driven, often oblivious to other people's feelings, and on a track of their own. When their vision is shared by a group, then they are often seen as heroes and leaders because they tend to forge ahead to meet challenges with unusual fearlessness. This style position by itself is extroverted and can withstand great stress. It does not favor artistic, aesthetic, or emotional modes of operating, but prefers a planned method for achieving goals and results.

218

Cognitive

This style dimension is characterized by a strong tendency to avoid negative influences from people or the environment. This type usually works best when goals are associated with, or requirements of, authority figures. Attention to details and being on the alert for potential dangers or inconsistencies enable individuals with this style to maintain a better position of security and control. People with this style tend to avoid emotional intensity and unpredictability, and they may especially need intimacy because they find it difficult to trust others. This style position by itself is introverted, being more sensitive to stimulation. It does not prefer sensory, emotional modes of operating, but tends toward logical analysis and correct performance of tasks, with an additional interest in the fine arts.

Interpersonal

This style dimension is characterized by a strong tendency to adapt to people and surroundings in order to promote harmony and comfort for self and others. Approaching people in a practical, friendly, and naturally warm manner is typical of this style dimension. Adaptation to all other styles is a way of life, providing the security desired and balance needed by those who score higher in this style dimension. A desire to support others in order to gain a sense of validation and approval is a natural tendency. This style position by itself is introverted, being more sensitive to stimulation. It favors a practical balance of both the logical and intuitive modes of functioning, thereby avoiding extremes. In this style there may also be a tendency toward stubbornness, especially if others are being overbearing.

Affective

This style dimension is characterized by a strong tendency to explore the environment intuitively and interact with it to assess the outcome. Spontaneous exploration and expression of ideas and feelings mark the natural tendencies of this style. People with an inclination toward this style dimension often attempt to influence others through creative media such as speaking, writing, dance, art, or music. They like to promote themselves and ideas or products that they believe will be helpful. They will go out of their way to help others even if it inconveniences them, because they believe in the value of people. By itself, this style is extroverted, not easily overstimulated by the environment. It does not favor the analytical modes of operating, but is more intuitive and creative in its way of functioning.

There's More to You Than These Scores Indicate

To start with, we'll deal with the scores you obtained when you took the PSI. It's important to appreciate that although these scores provide an indication of your personal style, they do not tell the whole story. There's more to you than your personal style, and there's more to personal style than is implied by the results you obtained when you took the PSI. There are four main reasons for this:

1. The PSI is not a test of any kind. You cannot fail it and you cannot pass it. It is simply an assessment of how you perceive your behavior.

2. Your scores on the PSI are only as accurate as your self-perception. In other words, if how you see yourself in relation to the self-descriptive words used in the indicator is distorted, then your scores will not accurately reflect your true personal style. For example, you may rate all of the affective words highly because you like to believe you're more expressive and creative than you really are. One of the best ways to obtain a more accurate score is to have several individuals who know you well complete the PSI response sheet. Ask them to rate your behavior. Then compare their perceptions of you with your own. Reality will most likely be found somewhere in-between of the two sets of results.

3. Your scores at any given time can be distorted by the mood you are in when you take the PSI. They also can be influenced by other factors such as the people you are with or recent events. But most people who repeat the PSI find their profile pattern remains the same, even though the score for each of the four dimensions may vary slightly.

4. Your scores can be influenced by unknown or subconscious factors. While it seldom happens, some individuals produce scores that seem quite unlike the person who they think they are.

    One student I worked with, for example, answered the indicator with responses that were completely at odds with her true personal style, as we later discovered. She was very confused when she saw her results. After discussing with me the characteristics of each of the different dimensions of personal style, she correctly found her strongest dimensions. We realized she had checked off items on the response sheet according to the way she had always wanted to be, not according to how she actually saw herself. After further discussion, it became evident that her ideal view of herself was based largely upon the kind of person her father wished she would be. By encouraging her to accept her "real" personal style and by then assisting her to let go of her father's expectations—which were a direct projection of his own style pattern anyway—I was able to use personal style theory to help her relinquish all those years of frustration during which she had tried to be someone she naturally could not be.

What your preferences indicate about you and how each dimension influences your behavior will be discussed as we move through the rest of the book. Keep a mental note of what your scores are or better yet, write them down on a piece of paper and keep them with you as you travel through the book. You are now ready to begin understanding what personal style is all about. Please turn to Chapter 1 and begin your journey!

Recommended Readings

Anderson, T. D. (1992). *Transforming leadership: New skills for an extraordinary future.* Amherst, Massachusetts: Human Resource Development Press, Inc.

Anderson, T. D., & Robinson, E. (1988). *The leader's manual for the Personal Style Indicator and the Job Style Indicator.* Abbotsford, BC: Consulting Resource Group International, Inc.

Anderson, T. D., & Robinson, E. (1987). *Personal Style Indicator.* Abbotsford, BC: Consulting Resource Group International, Inc.

Blitchington, W. P. (1983). *The energy and vitality book.* Wheaton, Illinois: Tyndale House Publishers, Inc.

Donovan, P., & Wonder, J. (1984). *Whole brain thinking.* New York, New York: William Morrow and Company.

Eysenck, H. J. (1963). The validity of questionnaire and rating assessments of extroversion and neuroticism, and their factorial stability. *British Journal of Psychology, 54,* 51-62.

Eysenck, H. J. (1970). *The structure of human personality.* London, England: Methuen and Co.

Eysenck, H. J., & Eysenck, M. (1983). *Mindwatching: Why people behave the way they do.* Garden City, New Jersey: Anchor Press, Doubleday.

Eysenck, H. J. (1990, April 30). An improvement on personality inventory. *Current Contents: Social and Behavioral Sciences, 22* (18), 423

Fromm, E. (1964). *The heart of man.* New York, New York: Harper and Row.

Galen (1981). *On the doctrines of Hippocrates and Plato* (2nd ed,; P. DeLacy, Trans.). Berlin, Germany: Akademie-Verlag.

Geier, J. (1977). *The personal profile system.* Performax Systems International, Inc.

Gottfredson, G. D., & Holland, J. L. (1989). *Dictionary of Holland Occupational Codes.* Odessa, Florida: Psychological Assessment Resources, Inc.

Herrman, N. (1990). *The creative brain.* Lake Lure, North Carolina: Brain Books.

Holland, J. L. (1973). *Making vocational choices: A theory of careers.* Englewood Cliffs, New Jersey: Prentice-Hall.

Horney, K. (1942). *Self-analysis.* New York, New York: Norton.

Johnson, C., Wood, R., & Blinkhorn, S. (1988). Spuriouser and spuriouser: The use of ipsative personality tests. *Journal of Occupational Psychology, 61*(2), 153-162.

Jung, C. (1923). *Psychological types.* London, England: Routledge.

Jung, C. (1928). *Contributions to analytic psychology.* New York, New York: New American Library.

Kouzes, J. M., & Posner, Barry Z. (1993). *Credibility.* San Francisco, California: Jossey-Bass.

LaHaye, T. (1966). *Spirit-controlled temperament.* Illinois: Tyndale House.

Lewin, K. (1936). *Principles of topological and vectoral psychology.* New York, New York: McGraw Hill.

Littauer, F. (1983). *Personality plus.* Michigan: Fleming H. Revell.

Littauer, F., & Littauer, M. (1992). *Personality puzzle.* Michigan: Fleming H. Revell.

Marston, W. (1927, July-Sept.). Motor consciousness as a basis for emotion. *Journal of Abnormal and Social Psychology,* XXII, 140-150.

Merrill, D., & Reid, R. (1981). *Personal styles and effective performance.* Radnor, Pennsylvania: Chilton Book Company.

Myers, D. (1989). *Psychology.* (1st and 2nd eds.). New York, New York: Worth.

Myers, I. & McCaulley, H. (1985). *Manual: A guide to the development and use of the Myers-Briggs Type Indicator.* Palo Alto, California: Consulting Psychologists Press.

Myers, I. B., & Myers, P. B. (1980). *Gifts differing.* Palo Alto, California: Consulting Psychologists Press, Inc.

Paltiel, L. (1986). Self-appraisal personality inventories. *Guidance and Assessment Review, 2*(3), 3-7.

Peters, T. J., & Waterman, R. H. (1982). *In search of excellence.* New York, New York: Harper & Row.

Robinson, E.T. (1987, January). Increasing self-worth during counselling: Personality factors to be considered. *Guidance and Counselling, 2* (3), 36-44.

Smalley, G., & Trent, J. (1990). *The two sides of love.* Pomona, California: Focus on the Family.

Thomas, A., & Chess, S. (1977). *Temperament and development.* New York, New York: Brunner-Mazel.

Wundt, W. (1904). *Principles of physiological psychology*, (Vol. 1; E.B. Tichener, Trans.). London: Swan, Sonnenschein.

Why Aren't You More Like Me? *is a dynamic book that immediately helped me understand the value of knowing various personality styles. Knowing how each personality type approaches a given set of criteria can make or break a business arrangement or a personal relationship. This understanding has assisted me in being more effective in my personal and business relationships. The presentation of the material in this book has been of utmost value to our organization. My sincere thanks to the author, Everett Robinson.*

Jim Janz, Chairman, Ambassador Business Network

Why Aren't You More Like Me? *provides valuable insight into understanding the fundamentals of relationship building, both with co-workers and family members. Finally there is a straight forward approach to solving the age-old problem of the "un-fixable personality conflict." The basic concept of understanding your personal style unlocks the key to successful interpersonal relationships.*

Mary Beth Henninger, Manager, Training and
Development, Conseco Companies

The return on our investment with Everett Robinson and the CRG instruments such as the PSI is amazing, it keeps on giving. Why Aren't You More Like Me? *by Everett, is in constant use by our managers, staff and now our clients. The value delivered by Everett and the PSI is the basis upon which we are a changed organization, it is now fundamental in our culture and part of who we are. The value goes beyond the company. Our employees use what they have learned and apply it in their personal lives, with their families, spouses and friends. I whole heartedly recommend the book and instruments to any and all who wish to bring about lasting change in their lives, relationships, and organizations.*

Robin McKinney, President, Northwest Digital Ltd.

I am really excited about the book, Why Aren't You More Like Me? *I have not read any book that I feel is so useful to me in my daily life. After reading this book many times, I can't think of a reason why anyone interested in improving their relationships with others would not really benefit. I really believe that if I had read this book 10 years ago I might have saved my marriage. This is a great book, please read it.*

Jim Castle, Independent Consultant

In Why Aren't You More Like Me?*, Everett Robinson provides a clear and concise explanation of personal style and its impact on all aspects of our lives. His book, along with its companion instrument, the Personal Style Indicator, formed the cornerstone of a workshop that was developed for the top 200 managers in GTE's East Area. Participants consistently commented about the positive insights the book helped them develop about their personal style and its impact on leadship.*

Michael E. Kossler, Manager-Organization
Development, GTE Telephone Operations, East Area